"There are lots of b[illegible]
developing, and deplo[illegible]
too many (if any) on doing the same thing with deacons. From Acts 6, Timothy 3, and Titus 1, it's abundantly clear that the deacon is a biblical office in the church. Why are they important? What role should they play? How do you find them? What about women deacons? Church planter and lead pastor Matt Ford has done his homework on this subject and practices what he writes about it at Restoration City Church in Hampton, Georgia. *That Deacon Book* is spot on! Here you will find material that is theologically sound, practical, and very relevant. Matt also incorporates research of deacons in early church history, which you will find intriguing, interesting, and encouraging. An added bonus is his great sense of humor. You're going to love this book! Do you need more leaders? Are the leaders you have overworked, and maybe over-committed? Having a band of deacons to help lift the load may be just what your church needs."

—**Dave Kraft**,
Author of *Leaders Who Last*,
Seminar Leader and Pastor

THAT DEACON BOOK

Hopefully, the least boring book
you'll ever read about deacons

Matt Ford

LUCIDBOOKS

That Deacon Book

Hopefully, the least boring book you'll ever read about deacons

Published by Lucid Books in Houston, TX.
www.LucidBooksPublishing.com

ISBN-10: 1632961245
ISBN-13: 9781632961242
eISBN-10: 1632961253
eISBN-13: 9781632961259

To Tim Bice and Kirk McDonald, my church-planting brothers and faithful friends.

And to Shannon, Maggie, Molly, and Martin, who share and sacrifice so much with husband and daddy for the gospel.

Contents

Preface

Howdy there. My name's Matt and I'm the church planting pastor of Restoration City Church (an Acts 29 church) in Hampton, Georgia.

"Hampton? Never heard of it," you say? Don't worry much about that. I'll fill you in. First, it's home to the Atlanta Motor Speedway (a big NASCAR track). Second, an episode of AMC's *The Walking Dead* was shot here. Sleepy little town, filled with sinners. I love it. It's been a real blast planting a church here.

God's been really awesome to me, my family, and our church. You'll hear me mention Restoration City Church (RCC) several times throughout the book. They're my favorite people in the world. Some of them are deacons, which is cool. They've all been *super*-generous in allowing me the time and energy to write this book.

I really hope this book is helpful to you and not the

least bit boring. I've aimed to be biblical, practical, and clear. I've prayed *a lot* that I would hit those targets.

So, let's get to reading and I'll see you on the other side. Actually . . . no. I'll see you on the next page, in the introduction, which you'd better read. Now, let's get to talking about deacons!

easier. Or maybe you've suddenly realized your church needs deacons and you want to know how to get the ball rolling in that direction. Whatever your perceptions and past experiences with deacons have been, I think this book can help you see just how important they are to a well-functioning church. In other words, I think you can really benefit from this book. I know that *I've* needed this book. In fact, that's one of the reasons I wrote it.

I'm a church planter who has recognized that not only do the Scriptures say that the church is to be *shepherded* by elders (there are many great resources for that), but also that the church is to have deacons in place to help *serve* the church body. As a church planter trying to figure out what deacons are supposed to do, I've often felt like I was one of those crazy kids in the *Lord of the Flies*, running around, trying to figure out the rules, and wondering if an adult was going to show up before I ended up smashing someone's head in with a rock. Strictly speaking, it was hard to find comprehensive instruction.

Thankfully, there are some good resources today about the role of deacons—articles from qualified churches, organizations, and pastors. And there are plenty of books on eldering that incorporate some teaching on the diaconate. But I needed—as have many of my fellow pastors—a comprehensive resource on biblical *deaconing*. Hence, this book.

Back to the Problem

Jesus starts his gospel message to us with some really bad news: you're sinful and deserve to be condemned. Thankfully, he doesn't leave us there. Instead, he serves us. He offers us the restorative, saving answer we need and can't get for ourselves. He willingly laid down his life for us in the most sacrificial way imaginable, taking on our sin and shame and giving us his forgiveness and righteousness. The best news in the history of the world starts with the worst news and ends with God's self-giving love. The gospel describes the servanthood of the only person who actually deserves to be served: Jesus.

With that said, there remains a problem (and it's not a new one): Jesus's church needs people to be like him by willingly serving others. Too often, the church is missing servants. I've heard about it, I've seen it, and I've experienced it firsthand. When churchgoers adopt a consumeristic mindset rather than a servant attitude, they'll look to have their needs met without considering how to meet the needs of others. This can result in pastors who are stretched thin by not only prayer, study, and preaching, but also such duties as administration, facility maintenance, hospital visits, and straightening up chairs in the worship area before the service. Nobody can keep all that up forever. A small and overworked staff of paid or unpaid leaders, carrying the weight of the entire church, is not God's plan for the church. Crowds of passive receivers with very few givers aren't sustainable or desirable. Churches are meant to be healthy, vibrant places where Christians serve one another in ways that strengthen the entire body to serve the community and the world. Church is meant to be a group project, and when that attitude (and practice) is lacking, it's because the church has a service problem. In short, it seems everyone wants to be near Jesus, learn about him, and even be like him. And yet, very few seem to want to live and die like him—in service to one another.

I don't want to mislead you here. I'm not offering up some new, innovative, patented idea that I came up with all on my own. I just want to serve you by showing you an important way God has designed for people to serve: deacons!

God's plan is for some Christians—*many* Christians—to step up and serve as deacons. That word is probably familiar to you if you've been around the church for any length of time, but I'm guessing it's not a regular topic of conversation. In a time when most churches have paid and unpaid staff as well as various directors, executives, associates, and lay leaders, it's my hope to draw us ever back to the Scriptures and see what God has already given us in the ministry of deacons. I don't want to get rid of all those other ministry titles, but to draw all of what we do together, under the design of God's Word.

I think I can already hear some of the misgivings

bouncing around in your head about deacons. Their role in the church has not been very well understood or appreciated. And, sadly, it has sometimes been abused, causing individuals and even entire churches a lot of pain. There have been some cases where the diaconate was laid out poorly and it felt like some deacon had received a title and a funny paper hat, and decided to throw their weight around. Nevertheless, the baby need not go out with the bathwater. So many problems in our world come from taking what God meant for our good, twisting it, doing damage, and then pointing at God's design as the problem. The Scriptures have something to say about the diaconate and how deacons are meant to be part of God's plan for joy, comfort, healing, stability, and flourishing in the church. So, it's not that the God-ordained office of deacon is broken or irrelevant; it's that we, as fallen men and women, are in need of constant reorientation and restoration to God's good design for the church and our lives.

Questions?

A pastor friend of mine will sometimes end meetings by asking, "Questions? Concerns? Declarations of heresy?" I've stolen that and used it a lot myself. Since I can't hear your questions, I'll try to at least anticipate some of them (and we'll all steer clear of declarations of heresy):

- Is this biblical? Where's this coming from and why should we care?

- Does my church really need deacons? Why can't we just have staff positions and keep it simple?
- Exactly who is supposed to be a deacon? Isn't everybody in the church supposed to be a servant?
- What is a deacon? What do they do that's different than what my pastor or elder does?
- Can women be deacons?
- How do I know if I should be a deacon? Is God calling me to be one?
- How can I become a deacon? Or, how do we get the office of deacon started in my church?
- What can I expect to change for me if I become a deacon, especially if I'm already serving my church?

Other Goals and Hints

I want us to learn what the Bible says about deacons, and I want to try to help us answer the questions above. My hope is we'll think and learn together and possibly share a chuckle or two (It is okay to chuckle while learning about deacons, right?). To that end, I've tried to write with a light touch about what I think is a pretty weighty subject.

So, take your time. Digest the material slowly. Write

notes. Pray. I've got questions for you to study and talk over with your pastor or elder—possibly with others who are learning about deacons. And be sure to go back and compare what I'm saying to the Bible. I teach the doctrine of *sola scriptura* to the people of my church, which is to say, Scripture alone is our highest authority. This book will never, and should never, be your final authority on the office of deacon. The Bible alone receives that honor. I've just tried to be faithful to it.

And one more thing before we get started: I don't know you, but I love you. (Jesus can have that effect on us!) I hope and pray that I'll be helpful to you. By God's grace, I will. Peace.

—Pastor Matt

July 2016

Chapter I
Why Deacons?

See what kind of love the Father has given to us, that we should be called the children of God; and so we are.
—1 John 3:1

So then you are no longer strangers and aliens, but you are fellow citizens with the saints and members of the household of God.
—Eph. 2:19

This Doesn't Feel like a Family

I know you've heard that before. If you've been part of a church, you've heard it. Honestly, I've even said it myself. We know something's wrong when church doesn't feel like a family, since the Bible portrays it as such (see Eph. 2:19). Even though many of my fellow pastors and I are tempted to lump people who complain this way into the "constant complainer" faction, I don't want us to become cynical about the possibility of a family-like atmosphere within our churches. Every church should, if it's a biblical church, act like a family.

Of course, there really are instances when someone will say that your church doesn't feel like a family and it's not anyone's fault but their own. They might simply be disengaged, uninformed, or just looking to find faults wherever they can. Often this attitude is a result of hurt from past sin and hurt from other churches. Certainly there are dysfunctional families out there, just as there can be an unfair critic in your church. Pastor John Piper once rightly described this sort of attitude and behavior as "emotional blackmail." The idea is that if I can accuse you of making me feel bad, I can get you to backpedal, apologize, and do what I tell you, even though you've done nothing wrong.[1] But if this dynamic prevails, issues don't actually get dealt with and nothing gets better as a result. So, if you are a brother pastor or leader, I urge you to serve these sheep patiently.

There was a time when I was one of those "constant

---

1. John Piper, "Piper on Emotional Blackmail in the Church," *The Gospel Coalition,* accessed June 8, 2016, https://blogs.thegospelcoalition.org/gospeldrivenchurch/2015/03/23/piper-on-emotional-blackmail-in-the-church/.

complainers." When I once said those words ("This doesn't feel like a family") at a church I'd been part of for six months, I got my rear end handed to me by the leader I said it to. I learned two valuable lessons:

- I don't always know what I'm talking about.
- It's not all about me.

What this leader lovingly and sternly told me was life-changing: "This church doesn't feel like a family to you? Why would it? You've been here for six months and you don't do or give anything here. It doesn't feel like a family because you treat it like a restaurant. You come here to get served and waited on rather than serving and waiting on others. Family members help each other out. Customers just show up, get stuff, and critique the service."

It was offensive to hear. And entirely true and necessary. At the time, it stung, and I didn't like it. But this leader loved me and the church enough to say the hard thing. A lot of people need to hear a kind yet pointed rebuke. The church does need to be a family, and the central, functional component of that family is serving one another—something which I wasn't yet committed to doing. That's where deacons (and this book) come in.

You might be saying to yourself as you read this, *My church feels like a family. We have many people serving. We have pastors, directors, executives, and administrators—we don't need deacons.* Everything you're thinking is probably accurate, except that last statement. *Every* church needs deacons. If your church feels like a family and nearly everyone is helping out, then you may very well have deacons. You just might not know it.

You might be tempted to think that's okay, but it's not. Without having an intentional diaconal ministry, we may stumble into something good for a while, but there's a good chance we'll eventually stumble back out of it. Besides, do we really want to toss out God's design and plan for his church, believing we can improve upon it?

I think a lot of the current American church thinks it can figure out new and better ways of doing church. We've believed that we can take God's design for his church, pick and choose the parts we like, and leave the rest out. I believe that we've been gradually introducing unnecessary difficulty into the church by trying to "update" God's design for how things should work. The church does need to constantly consider ways to innovate, but not ways that go against or ignore how God has explicitly designed his church. That's not to say we can't innovate on how to implement God's plan, but we can't afford to neglect or opt out of what he's laid down for us.

Many churches have looked to American corporate business structures over the last few decades and rightly said, "Maybe we can learn from that." Sadly, much of the American church didn't just learn, but adopted most of the governing structures of the corporate world, tossing vital parts of God's structure into the trashcan of history. Things like elders, deacons, and covenant membership have come to be seen as too old-fashioned and outdated. *Modern people don't care about those things. Those offices and structures aren't relevant anymore. They don't help us grow the church exponentially and dynamically.* Or, at least, that's what a lot of us thought.

Pointing Out the Problem

I'm from the American south, so many of us are familiar with the prototypical plumber named Bubba, his low-hanging jeans revealing back-side things you can't un-see, holding a major problem up in front of our faces, saying, "See, here's your problem!" We have to assess the problems, which can be pretty rough. But it's necessary. That'll lead us to seeing why God's design isn't just good, but necessary, and departing from it really detracts from the health of our churches.

The problem started way back in Genesis 1-3. In the beginning, God made it all and he said it was *good.* We tend to read through that stuff way too quickly. God didn't just create all the stuff in the universe. He created all the definitions for that stuff. He established a purpose and design for how everything is supposed to work. That's still true despite the fall and sin, especially in God's redemptive vehicle, the church. In the beginning, everything worked right and it worked together. This is partially what the ancient Hebrews meant by the term *shalom*. It means that everything and everyone are working in unified peace in exactly the way God meant them to. We ignore his plan and design at our own peril. Everything *was* perfect in its *being* and everything worked together perfectly in its *doing*.

Imagine you're the guy who invented the chainsaw. You conceived in your mind an amazing power tool for the expressed purpose of cutting down trees and chopping up logs. Before you actually created the first chainsaw, you determined, as the inventor, what it was for. Now, imagine the horror you would feel if you discovered that someone was planning to use it to do dental work.

Hey, buddy! You can't take a chainsaw to that guy's jaw! That's not what it's for!" you shout.

"Yeah?" retorts the indignant murderer-dentist, "That's just your opinion, man. It's my chainsaw. I'll do what I want with it!"

You want to snatch the chainsaw out of his hands, right? He's about to do some serious damage. Clearly, this guy should not be practicing dentistry with a chainsaw. You should know; you designed it. You know that it's for trees, not teeth.

Now, take that whole scenario and replace *chainsaw* with *church* and you'll understand how God must feel sometimes. When God conceived of the church, he established patterns and structures for how it's supposed function. We're in the best possible position to enjoy and reap God's blessings in the church when we obey his design for it without trying to improve upon it. Conversely, we run the risk of doing great damage when we stray from God's intentions. Of course, there continue to be advances in dental equipment and probably even chainsaws. Technology created by imperfect people can always be improved upon. However, when it comes to God and his Word, we are dealing with perfection. He designed the church as it should be, right from the start. So, our churches need deacons if we want to do things God's way.

The "Why" Is the Gospel

In the Gospel of Matthew, two of Jesus's buddies, James and John, get their mom to ask Jesus to put them in the "assistant-god" position in his kingdom. Jesus tells her, "You do not know what you are asking. . . . Whoever would be great among you must be your servant, and whoever would be first among you must be your slave, even as the Son of Man came not to be served but to serve, and to give his life as a ransom for many" (Matt. 20:22, 26-28).

Jesus tells us that he, the King of kings and Lord of lords, made it his primary mission to serve others. The only one who's truly worthy of being served came to serve by laying his life down for us. *This* is the bottom-line reason—the "why" of incorporating the office of deacon into our churches.

If I wrote a book on deacons and told you that the "why" was bigger offerings on Sundays, more excitement, greater numerical growth, and a joyful, flourishing church community, I'd be doing you a terrible disservice. Granted, I believe that governing a church by God's design will generally result in greater or lesser growth in those areas. But those things aren't the "why" of this book on deacons.

Don't get me wrong: those things are great! I celebrate those kinds of "growth metrics" in the church, including in my own church. We *should* dream of, pray for, and strive toward those things. The problem is when those good things become separated from a motivation to walk in God's design, they can easily become worldly objectives. The glory and splendor of the Jesus, "in whom all the fullness of God was pleased to dwell" (Col. 2:9), takes a back seat to worldly "success." What we end up worshiping and chasing after is no longer God's glory alone, but the glory of our churches and ministry careers. No longer will Jesus be "the head of the body, the church" (Col. 1:18), as the church won't be centered on his glory anymore, but on its own. And we'll end up doing whatever it takes to get what we're after, even if it doesn't fit with God's good and wise design.

We've got to get this motivation—this gospel

motivation—firmly rooted in our hearts and minds. God's design for his church, including the office of deacon, is to glorify himself and put his goodness, wisdom, grace, and righteousness on display to a fallen world in need of salvation. Our churches should have deacons, whether or not it results in greater attendance. I'm not going to tell you to install people as deacons because it's the "secret" that's going to "take your church to the next level." I'm telling you to do it because it's biblical and because it's how God says the church should operate. Deacons reflect Jesus's servant heart. They glorify him and make the gospel more attractive and inviting.

I certainly believe that when churches walk in God's design, good things are more likely to occur, especially in a robust, healthy, long-term way. God appears to have prescribed the ministry of deacons as a way through which the Holy Spirit works powerfully, often resulting in greater numbers of people coming to saving faith, deeper discipleship, and greater generosity. But I'd rather have less of these things in obedience to God, than more through disobedience. In the long run, getting "results" without obedience is never worth it.

The Gospel on Display

How does the office of deacon do all that God-glorifying stuff? The center of the Christian church is the gospel message. It's the soul-saving, life-transforming news that Jesus has left his eternal home in heaven and entered into human history as a man. The King, the only person worthy of being served and honored, came down from his throne to serve us. Exactly what was the nature of his service?

The Book of Isaiah (53:1-12) describes the sort of service that Jesus would perform for us:

- He bore our griefs, suffering the soul-anguish we experience.
- He carried our sorrows, empathizing and sympathizing with us.
- He was pierced for our transgressions, chastened, and scourged, offering his physical body to receive the physical pain and condemnation we deserve as enemies of God.
- He took upon himself our sin and iniquity so that we could be counted as righteous and pure.

Jesus, though he is God, "did not count equality with God a thing to be grasped, but emptied himself, by taking on the form of a servant, being born in the likeness of men" (Phil. 2:6, 7). The pinnacle of Jesus's service was to obey his heavenly Father—he was "obedient to the point of death, even death on a cross" (Phil. 2:8). He served us through both his life and death.

When the church thinks and lives like Jesus—that is,

when we serve one another—we put the gospel on display for one another and for the world. That's exactly what the church should be doing in every arena: *putting the gospel on display.* When we're saved by Jesus, we're saved into his family. We receive the indwelling Holy Spirit. Our old spiritual DNA is overwritten by our new spiritual DNA. Like little brothers and sisters of Jesus, we imitate him because we have his life inside of us (cf. Gal. 2:20).

The Tip of the Spear

Some of you might still be wondering why we need all this talk about deacons, since every Christian is called to serve. While it's true that the Greek word *diakonos* simply means "servant," and every Christian *is* called to serve, there remains an important distinction between the office of deacon and an everyday Christian who serves. Deacons aren't just supposed to serve; they're supposed to *lead* the rest of the church in service by their faithful example.

Further into this book, I'll also cover some of the distinctions between deacons and elders. For now, you need to know that gospel-displaying deacons in the church are *leaders*. Their leadership role is different than that of an elder, but still critically important. At my church, we've created a shorthand way of differentiating the two offices:

- Elders are servant-leaders.
- *Deacons are lead servants.*

When it comes to serving, deacons are the tip of the spear. They're the first to jump, first to volunteer, first to give, and first to try new things out. Like in the Marine Corps, deacons are the gunnery sergeants—leading, managing, and training the Christians around them in service, all the while offering a faithful biblical example of service. It's not enough to tell people they must serve like Jesus. We've got to *show* them how to serve like Jesus. For this purpose, Jesus has given us the office of deacon.

The "Why" Is Vital

I've read my fair share of Christian books—books on pastoring, on kids' ministry, on discipleship. And in every book that's worth reading, the author always lays out the "why"—the theology that drives everything they're saying. I confess that I'm tempted to skip it or skim it, assuming I don't need to pay attention since I already know all that gospel stuff. Nevertheless, our theology drives the way we live our lives and serve our churches. Implementing or reorganizing the *diaconate* in your church will—*I guarantee it*—require a lot of thinking, planning, vision-casting, teaching, question-answering, and pushback management. It'll require a constant return to the Scriptures. And, for the most part, you want it this way. Constructive feedback from your elders and leaders will help shape the best implementation you can get. You might have every organizationally minded leader in your church wanting to know all the details and implications of how this plays out. And if you have an existing church that's been around for more than a year or two, there could be a lot of whiteboarding, brainstorming, and discussion that needs to take place.

That's why the "why" is so vital to understand. Implementation could get a little complicated. It'll likely test your patience. But, it's when the going gets tough that you'll really need the "why" to keep you on track and motivated to see this through. A church with a biblical diaconate reflects the gospel more fully, walks in closer biblical faithfulness, and is more effectively on mission for God.

Chapter 2
What's a Deacon?

Now in these days when the disciples were increasing in number, a complaint by the Hellenists arose against the Hebrews because their widows were being neglected in the daily distribution. And the twelve summoned the full number of the disciples and said, "It is not right that we should give up preaching the word of God to serve tables. Therefore, brothers, pick out from among you seven men of good repute, full of the Spirit and of wisdom, whom we will appoint to this duty. But we will devote ourselves to prayer and to the ministry of the word." And what they said pleased the whole gathering, and they chose Stephen, a man full of faith and of the Holy Spirit, and Philip, and Prochorus, and Nicanor, and Timon, and Parmenas, and Nicolaus, a proselyte of Antioch. These they set before the apostles, and they prayed and laid their hands on them. And the word of God continued to increase, and the number of the disciples multiplied greatly in Jerusalem, and a great many of the priests became obedient to the faith.

—Acts 6:1-7

Servants or Formal Office?

In the previous chapter, I said that every Christian is meant to be a servant. That being said, there appears to be a specific distinction in the Scriptures between a person in the church who serves and a person who holds the office of deacon.[2]

The majority of instances in the New Testament where the Greek word *diakonos* is used actually refer, quite simply, to servants rather than the office of deacon. Consider the following references:

- **Luke 22:26, 27:** "Let the greatest among you become as the youngest, and the leader as one who serves (*diakonon*). . . . I am among you as the one who serves (*diakonon*)."
- **John 12:26:** "If anyone serves (*diakone*) me, he must follow me; and where I am, there will my servant (*diakonos*) be also."
- **Ephesians 3:7:** "Of this gospel I was made a minister (*diakonos*) according to the gift of God's grace, which was given me by the working of his power."
- **1 Timothy 4:6:** "If you put these things before the brothers, you will be a good servant

2. See Bob Thune, "Deacons: A Theological Study," accessed June 13, 2016, http://bobthune.s3.amazonaws.com/Deacons_%20A_Theological_Study.pdf.

> (*diakonos*) of Christ Jesus, being trained in the words of the faith and of the good doctrine that you have followed."

Nevertheless, in Philippians 1:1, Paul mentions elders and deacons together, and in 1 Timothy 3:8, he lists the character qualifications for the office of deacon. In both instances, the term *diakonos* is used in a narrower sense to refer specifically to the office of deacon.

I've never been a great math student. For example, regardless of how many geometry classes I've been tortured with, I've never understood how anyone could argue that pies are square. They're *pies*; they're round. As far as geometric shapes go, though, I *do* know that all squares are rectangles, but not all rectangles are squares. Similarly, all deacons are servants, but not all servants are deacons.

To further establish the distinction between the general and narrow use of the term *diakonos,* I want to point out that the qualifications for deacons are practically duct-taped to the qualifications for elders. It seems apparent and reasonable that the diaconate is an office in the same sense that elders are an office within the church. In the above reference to 1 Timothy 3, Paul greets the saints in Christ (the members), then the elders, and then the deacons—a distinct group, like the elders, mentioned along with the members of the church.

Finally, 1 Timothy 3 provides quite specific character qualifications that a person needs to demonstrate in order to be considered for the office of deacon. One might say (rightly, too!) that these qualifications aren't simply for deacons, but for all Christians. Yes, absolutely. All Christians should strive to have these character traits (dignified, not double-tongued, sober-minded, etc.). But these character traits are, again, listed immediately after the character traits required for a man to be an elder, and not every Christian man holds the office of elder. Nor does every Christian hold the office of deacon.

The Office of Deacon, Part 1: Historical Origin

In Acts 6, the brand-new Christian church in Jerusalem faced its first major problem. I'm sure the apostles, the first pastors, were frustrated by the fact that the "brand-new car" smell of the church was wearing off so quickly.

There was division in the church—big time.[3] The Christians who'd lived their lives in Jewish culture, speaking the Jewish language, observing Jewish laws and customs, were being taken care of first, while the Greek-speaking, Greek-cultured, ethnically Jewish Christians were being taken care of last. This primarily meant that most of the food and money the church was donating

3. If anyone ever says to you, "Our church should get back to being an 'Acts 2' church," fight the urge to beat them up. If your church has problems, congratulations! You're already on your way to being an "Acts 2" church.

to the older women, widows, and orphans was actually being poured into one group, and another group was getting little-to-nothing.

Huge problem, right? The apostles knew it needed to be dealt with. But, in pastoral wisdom, they recognized that the church didn't need them to leave Bible study, prayer, and preaching to go to the distribution center and start taking inventory, making sure that everything was fair and that everyone got enough.

What the church didn't need the pastors to do was to stop doing what only they can do—that is, serve the church through prayer and Holy Spirit–empowered preaching of the Word. What the church did need was qualified, godly servants—people who knew how to serve, had a commitment to serve, and knew how to lead others in the church to serve—to handle these ground-level needs of the church.

So, what theologians often refer to as the *proto-diaconate* was established. Seven men of "good repute, full of the Spirit and of wisdom" were chosen to serve the church in a specific manner with some level of authority. Stephen, Philip, Prochorus, Nicanor, Timon, Parmenas, and Nicolaus served as prototypes for the office of deacon. These men were put before the apostles, implying that the church knew these men and no one had anything of significance to say that would disqualify them from wielding influence and authority. The apostles laid hands on them and prayed over them, establishing what would later be identified as the formal office of deacon. That's why these six men are referred to as the *proto-diaconate.* Acts 6 doesn't actually use the noun *diakonos*—but it is here that a distinction is created that would lead to the diaconate.

What was the result of the institution of these proto-deacons in the church? Acts 6:7 says that the "Word of God continued to increase," meaning that the Bible was preached with no distraction or divergence by the pastors who were free to focus on that and only that. When the preaching of the Word of God increases, the people of God are "equipped for every good work" (2 Tim. 3:17), they grow in the wisdom of God as the word of Christ dwells in them richly (Col. 3:16), and they worship more deeply, having seen him more clearly.[4]

The church also saw the number of disciples increase—this is a biblical *description*, I have to note, rather than a biblical *guarantee* of what happens when you walk in God's design for the church. Some churches, as well as some Christians, walk in tremendous obedience to the Lord's will, with clear consciences, and things do not go well for them. Jesus said John the Baptist was the greatest man ever born (Matt. 11:11), and he spent the final months of his life in prison and had his head lopped off

---

4. Jonathan Edwards, *The Miscellanies: The Works of Jonathan Edwards, No. 448.*

by a wicked king. God has never required success from his people. He calls us to faithfulness, regardless of how well it works out.

In any case, there was now a more organized structure within the church—order that helped make sure that what the church needed was supplied. God's Word was preached by those who should preach it, the church was governed by the elders, and the church was served by the body with these six men leading with good character and their good example.

In fact, this passage ends with the statement that "many of the (Jewish) priests became obedient to the faith" (Acts 1:7). Even hyper-religious people can have their eyes opened and their ears unstopped to receive saving faith. It helps when the church of Jesus's gospel is well-taught, well-led, and well-served. In this case, God chose to accomplish all these things through his human agents acting in accordance with his design for the church.

The Office of Deacon, Part 2: A Brief Etymological Study

I think we should know as much as we can about how God designed the church, so we can obey him as much as we can. Language—specifically, what we call things—is so vital. Some think that debates over semantics and nomenclature are nothing but worthless distractions. I understand that sentiment and I mostly agree. I've never gotten that giddy over doing etymological studies. But, we have a God who speaks to us! When he speaks, he has specific things he means and the names he gives to things are the names we should use. Ideas and concepts (like justice, grace, love, peace, acceptance) are getting more and more confused in our modern day, and I believe a lot of the confusion and tension is coming from poor definitions or, worse, redefining terms that God has already authoritatively defined.

So, we have the term *deacon*, which comes from the Greek word, *diakonos* (with related terms like the verb, *diakoneo* [to serve] and the noun, *diakonia* [ministry, service]). We've already seen that, in its predominant use in the New Testament, *diakonos* simply refers to servants. In addition, we've also recognized that there is an additional, narrower use of the term, identifying a specific office in the church—established in a prototypical phase in Acts 6. Somewhere in the church-planting process of the Book of Acts—and we don't know precisely where or when—the *diakonos* became a formal office (with character qualifications in 1 Timothy 3 and a mention by the apostle Paul in his greetings in Philippians 1).

But why should we call people who lead in servant ministry *deacons*? Why not just use the titles we've come up with over the last few decades? Children's director. Financial administrator. Ministerial advisor. Outreach coordinator. I don't think those are bad terms. I don't think we have to throw them out. Later on, I'll discuss what we might do with those titles. But for the moment, I believe we should still use and teach our churches the theology and practical application of the *diaconate*.

Why? It's the term God's Word uses. No true Christian would ever suggest that we think we can actually improve on God's Word or his designs. But the path to departing from God's ways starts with small divergences. When we start governing and organizing the church outside of the authority of Scripture, things tend to get more confusing, not less. In the long term, the weakening of scriptural structures and language results in manmade structures and terminology—and it'll go really badly for us leaders who either purposefully or ignorantly lead God's people away from the clarity and authority of his Word. We should all desire and strive to plant, lead, and enjoy churches that are as biblically faithful as possible—churches that align with God's Word in every way.

Servant-Leaders and Lead Servants

As I said earlier, in my church, we've adopted language from what we believe we see in the Bible, referring to what elders and deacons are. It's shorthand for the interplay and relationship between both offices:

- Elders are servant-leaders.
- Deacons are lead servants.

In many fundamentalist, primarily Baptist, churches,

the governing body of the church (the primary, authoritative leadership) is found in a collective board of deacons. The only problem we should have with that is what the Bible says about church governance. God has clearly said the governing of the church is to be done by a council of elders, not deacons. Many will refer to this office with a variety of biblical terms: "pastors," "bishops," "overseers," or "shepherds." Throughout the New Testament Scriptures, certainly, these terms interchangeably for the same position. I generally tend to use the terms "pastor" or "elder."[5]

An elder isn't a deacon and a deacon isn't an elder. They're not the same thing and they have different responsibilities and purposes. They are meant to work in a complimentary way, however. While the elders are called to direct the affairs of the church (1 Tim. 5:17), deacons are called to facilitate and manage the affairs of the church, as we saw in Acts 6. While elders are primarily called to lead the ministry, deacons are primarily called to execute the ministry, leading the rest of the church in the work.

In this way, we see that elders serve the church through praying and meditating on God's Word, and then preaching, teaching, counseling, and deliberating on the

5. The gold standard for studying biblical eldership is Alexander Strauch's *Biblical Eldership: An Urgent Call to Restore Biblical Church Leadership.*

major affairs of the church. Deacons, at the direction and under the guidance and authority of the elders, execute the good works of the church as a response to the preached Word of God.

For now, let's just say that deacons, in the course of leading the church in service, may perform in functions that are more or less visible, more or less "important," and more or less desirable. Some deacons will serve in minor roles and others will serve in roles with greater influence. The deacon is a Christian in the church who leads by example in their Christian walk and in their faithful work for the church ministry. A deacon is a Christian the church should be able to direct any member to and say, "Imitate him. Imitate her. Imitate them as they imitate Jesus" (see 1 Cor. 11:1).

Chapter 3

Who Are the Deacons?

Deacons likewise must be dignified, not double-tongued, not addicted to much wine, not greedy for dishonest gain. They must hold the mystery of the faith with a clear conscience. And let them also be tested first; then let them serve as deacons if they prove themselves blameless. Their wives likewise must be dignified, not slanderers, but sober-minded, faithful in all things. Let deacons each be the husband of one wife, managing their children and their own households well. For those who serve well as deacons gain a good standing for themselves and also great confidence in the faith that is in Christ Jesus.

—1 Tim. 3:8-13

Character before Competency

The American church's system of leadership selection seems to be based on achievement and skill. There's nothing wrong with achievement and skill—indeed, good leaders get results and must have the necessary skills to do the work. We should find it a bit troubling, however, that our leaders tend to be chosen first on the basis of ability when the Bible doesn't start there at all.

Who hasn't heard of this or that big-time pastor or leader who left his wife and ran away with the church pianist? Or, the one who stole a ton of money from the church? Or the one who did both? Or the one who did or said unprintable things? The modern church—at least in America—has a leadership problem. We don't lack capable, skilled leaders. We lack biblically qualified, godly leaders. Three common areas of disqualifying sin church leaders succumb to relate to the mishandling of money, sex, and power; it takes a leader with godly character, filled with the Holy Spirit to resist and flee from these temptations.

Some leaders are disqualified and must step aside because of an addiction to pornography or because they have committed adultery. Others steal money or are greedy for too much gain. Still others must step aside (or be forced out) because of a domineering or controlling leadership style. These moral failings not only hurt the leader and his or her family, but they also hurl the local church into a pit of trust-destroying confusion, damage the credibility of the church in the eyes of the lost, and worst of all, they assault the righteous and holy reputation of Jesus.

You don't even have to look at the church. Just pay attention to the young superstars drafted at the age of nineteen and twenty into the NBA, NFL, or MLB. Men with incredible talent—mythical golden boys and prodigies. They become famous and wealthy overnight. Entire clubs and fan bases put their hopes and dreams on these guys. A young man will suddenly have thousands of adoring fans, many of them women, who are willing to do whatever it takes to get close to him and get his favor. Time and time again, our society has seen this kind of quick success crush these men right before our eyes. They're either going to entertain us with their athletic feats, or they're going to entertain us with their personal downfall. The lesson we aren't teaching to young men and women is that your ability can take you to a place that your character can't maintain. Your skills can place you on a pedestal so high and narrow that you don't have the focus and balance to stand on it for long.

That's why God's plan for identifying leaders—in this case, deacons—starts not with competency, but with character. The question isn't just "Does this person understand what a deacon is and can they do the job?" The question is, "Is this the kind of person who should be a deacon?" For this reason, the Apostle Paul warns Timothy not to "be too hasty in the laying on of hands," which is to say, "don't raise someone to leadership who's untested, has hidden or unrepentant sin, or who hasn't shown themselves to have godly character."[6]

Again, let's not swing the pendulum too far to the other side. I'm not saying that a deacon (or any leader) doesn't need to have competency in some way—they *should* have competency in the area where they're serving. I don't want to create the mentality that a guy with *just* a "good heart" should be made a leader of some sort. That's just the opposite of the problem I spoke of above—in this case, you have someone who's got the character to handle success, they just don't have the ability to achieve it.[7] Many of us have had the encounter with the dear, sweet, godly lady in the church who has a deep passion to sing on stage with the worship team—but even though her voice is a truly joyful noise in the ear of the Lord, to us it sounds like someone's strangling a manatee.

Part of God's calling to a particular ministry or action

---

6. 1 Tim. 5:22. The surrounding context concerns dealing with sin and accusations of sin in church leaders.

7. Let's recognize that if an unskilled or untrained person is truly called by God to a task or office, our Father, who gives all needed things to his children, will supply skill—that, or they'll receive the necessary help needed in order to obey the calling. Consider the stuttering public speaking skills of Moses in Exodus 4, and God's provision of his brother Aaron, who spoke well.

will often require a competency that goes with the calling. In his excellent book *Am I Called?*, Dave Harvey rightly states that if a man can't preach, he's not called to be a lead pastor.[8] If you can't throw, you're not called to pitch. If you can't see, you're not called to pilot a plane or perform surgery. If you can't . . . well, you get the idea.

With that qualification, I reiterate: God has shown us, in the Scriptures, that character is of first importance—even before ability—when it comes to appointing leaders like elders and deacons.

Putting Character to the Test

One of the toughest things I've had to learn as a pastor is how to discern a person's character—starting with my own. When I felt called to be a church-planting pastor, I knew I couldn't move forward with just the feeling that I'm called. I knew my character had to be evaluated, since, again, the primary qualifications for pastors are character qualifications. The difficulty was, as it often still is: I both know myself and *don't* know myself.

Jeremiah 17:9 says, "The heart is deceitful above all things, and desperately sick; who can understand it?" The most difficult heart to understand is my own. How many times have I sat and tried to examine my motivations before making a decision? How many times have you? Often, we feel like we can read other people's hearts, minds, and

8. Dave Harvey, *Am I Called?* (Wheaton, IL: Crossway, 2012).

circumstances better than our own. So much of the time we see a clear way of thinking and handling our friend's problems. But if you turn it around and the problem is yours, the world suddenly becomes a mythological Greek labyrinth, complete with minotaurs hunting you down.

So, when I try to judge my own character, I'll be tempted to either overestimate or underestimate both my good and bad qualities. The minute I think, *Hey, I'm an honest guy,* a small, distant (or recent!) past lie will creep up in my memory, and now I feel like I'm a big, fat liar. When I try to discern what kind of a man I am on my own, I'm either the kind of guy that Charles Haddon Spurgeon[9] would seek out for coaching, or I'm disqualified from all ministry, for all time.

So, I'm stuck. My heart will lie to me! How can I tell if I have the character for what I think God's calling me to do? How do I get off this crazy seesaw of my own character analysis?

Another problem is we've all had a person in our lives whom we get to know and think is terrific—we're ready to vouch for them to be a children's ministry volunteer or date our sister—and then, surprisingly, they turn out to be not who we thought they were. We ask ourselves *How could I have been so blind? How did I let them fool me with their flattery or with their fake morality?*

---

9. Charles Haddon Spurgeon (1834-1892), the "Prince of Preachers." Another legendary guy who opened the Bible and preached the gospel faithfully and with great power. Look him up.

How can we know someone's character? If we're supposed to install and train leaders like deacons in the church, they must have their character tested. At this point, someone's going to say, "Well, you can't ever know for sure. So, we just leave it up to the Lord." That person's right, in a way. After denouncing the deceitful hearts of men in verse 9, the book of Jeremiah goes on to say (in verse 10), "I the LORD search the heart and test the mind, to give every man according to his ways, according to the fruit of his deeds." Yes, we leave it to the Lord—but that doesn't mean simply closing our eyes, hoping for the best, and believing that some sort of vague, spiritual enlightenment will land on us. The Lord probably won't see fit to visit you in the form of a hazy, blue ghostlike Obi-Wan Kenobi and tell you that ole' Jimmy, your deacon candidate, is a swell guy.

So, how does the Lord, who reads the hearts of men, help us discern someone's character? In brief: *character is revealed over time, in Christian community*. When I determined to seek help in confirming my call to plant a church, I followed the advice and example of my friend Kirk. He'd just spent the better part of two months working through the evidence in his life that God had called him to plant a church. When it came to character, I sought him, other godly pastors, and wise, mature Christians who'd spent a lot of time with me—people who'd seen me work, seen me play, seen me at my best, and seen me at my worst. These trusted people had observed me as I pursued righteousness, and they'd seen me repent of my sin. They'd all had enough time to see me in a variety of seasons of life that people go through.

I asked them to look at the character qualifications for a pastor in 1 Timothy 3 and consider my character through that lens. I asked them, "Do you, to the best of your prayerful discernment, believe that my character qualifies as the character of a pastor? If not, in what ways?" This was a community of believers—folks who got to see me from different angles (my leaders, people who followed me, my peers, family); these were folks who got to see me over time. They could read Scriptures like Galatians 5:16-24 to see if my life bore demonstrable evidence—the fruit of the Spirit—that I am one who "belongs to Christ Jesus" having "crucified the flesh with its passions and desires."

God's got a great system in place for Christians to test their character—over time, in community. We can see the big picture of this protocol in the New Testament Scriptures. They speak to God's intention that we are to live in close, knowing community, keeping watch on our souls and one another's:

- **Hebrews 10:24, 25**: "And let us consider how to stir up one another to love and good works, not neglecting to meet together, as is the habit of some, but encouraging one another, and all the more as you see the Day drawing near."

- **Galatians 6:1-3**: "Brothers, if anyone is caught in any transgression, you who are spiritual should restore him in a spirit of gentleness. Keep watch on yourself, lest you too be tempted. Bear one another's burdens, and so fulfill the law of Christ. For if anyone thinks he is something, when he is nothing, he deceives himself."
- **Colossians 2:1-5**: "For I want you to know how great a struggle I have for you and for those at Laodicea and for all who have not seen me face to face, that their hearts may be encouraged, being knit together in love, to reach all the riches of full assurance of understanding and the knowledge of God's mystery, which is Christ, in whom are hidden all the treasures of wisdom and knowledge. I say this in order that no one may delude you with plausible arguments. For though I am absent in body, yet I am with you in spirit, rejoicing to see your good order and the firmness of your faith in Christ."

Each of these passages describes a community of believers who, in their shared love of Jesus and in their shared salvation under the gospel, look after one another in the pursuit of godliness. The evidence of godliness is godly character. And that's best judged, it seems, by those who see you up close and personal over a period of time.

Dave Harvey has something brilliant to say about calling on other Christians in the church to take part in the confirmation of a minister's calling:

> In a real sense, the whole church is part of the confirmation process. You live and minister among folks who know you and have opinions about you. If you're a saint in front of the elders and a jerk to everybody else, your chances of [leadership] confirmation are microscopic. Now, the goal isn't to live life auditioning for the ministry. It's to live your life loving God and others in a way that will increasingly affect people in the way a pastor should affect them.[10]

Each candidate should be one who leaders and members of the church have known in deep community for some wisely established period of time. How long is that? I have no idea for your church. At my church, we have a general sense that the earliest we consider someone's character for deacon candidacy is three or four months. With that said, we could progress earlier if the person really seems to be demonstrating godliness in consistent ways; we might move more slowly with a person we've known longer if there are any concerning patterns of sin.

---

10. Harvey, *Am I Called?*, 172.

The determination of how much time a church needs to establish a credible sense of a leader's character must rest firmly on the shoulders of the qualified, Spirit-empowered elders. After all, I can't just give you *all* the answers, right? (I say that with my tongue firmly planted in my cheek.)

That might seem like a lot to go through—that is, until you experience the great pain and damage that a leader with poor character can do. Good ole Ben Franklin once said, "An ounce of prevention is worth a pound of cure." There are things you can't prevent, no matter what. But we can't afford to shirk our responsibilities as leaders and shepherds to guard the flock from harmful leaders who have poor character.

The Character of a Deacon

So, what kind of a person is a deacon? I've been trying to nail this one firmly to the wall because it matters. At Restoration City Church, all our elders and deacons know that before we care about what they're *doing* for Christ, we care about who they *are* in Christ. What are we looking for? First Timothy 3 is our text:

> Deacons likewise must be dignified, not double-tongued, not addicted to much wine, not greedy for dishonest gain. They must hold the mystery of the faith with a clear conscience. And let them also be tested first; then let them serve as deacons if they prove

themselves blameless. Their wives likewise must be dignified, not slanderers, but sober-minded, faithful in all things. Let deacons each be the husband of one wife, managing their children and their own households well. For those who serve well as deacons gain a good standing for themselves and also great confidence in the faith that is in Christ Jesus.

Let's parse this passage out in a bullet list:

- **Deacons are dignified:** Some translations will render the word for "dignified" as "grave" or "serious," coming from the Greek word used, *semnos*. This characteristic means "weighty," "majestic," and having a certain *gravitas*. This doesn't mean a deacon can't have a sense of humor—deacons aren't barred from having fun. But a deacon is a person who can rightly recognize the difference between solemn and happy circumstances. This is someone who doesn't have to demand respect, because his attitude and demeanor simply command it. While able to laugh and play, they're not considered to be silly; they're not immature.
- **Deacons aren't double-tongued:** In Greek, the descriptive word is *dilogos*. This can easily be understood to mean gossiper—someone who will speak kindly to your face, but

unkindly behind your back (We're lookin' at you, Real Housewives of Beverly Hills!). In a deeper, possibly more significant sense, this is a person whose word is reliable and trustworthy. They speak with integrity. They're honest. Their "yes" means yes and their "no" means no. They know when to hold their tongues and maintain their trust as confidants (read James 3).

- **Deacons aren't addicted to too much wine:** Clearly, I am a person with lots to say—but I won't take the time here to cover what my church's biblically based position on wine is; that's for each church's elders to weigh, according to the Scriptures. In this case, the deacon is cautious and guarded in his consumption of wine. Whether the deacon is having a little vino to settle his stomach,[11] or if he's sharing a six-pack with friends around the fire pit, he doesn't flirt with stepping over the line into drunkenness. Paul used the word *presecho* to describe the attitude a deacon needs to avoid regarding alcohol—that is, he isn't preoccupied with it. He doesn't need it. It's not the most important, comfort-bringing aspect of his day. It doesn't hold sway over his

11. Paul's advice to Timothy in 1 Timothy 5:23.

health, wealth, or work. And please, please, dear deacon—don't drink wine from a box. That just ain't right.

- **Deacons aren't greedy for dishonest gain:** Love the term "filthy lucre." Sounds like the stage name of a *luchador* (a Mexican professional wrestler). "In this corner, tag-team wrestling's newest sensation, Nacho Libre and Filthy Lucre!" Deacons can't be thieves—they need to be trusted with the resources of the church. They have to be trustworthy in this area as much of their work will involve money or materials meant for distribution to the people of the church. I'll paraphrase Jesus: "If you can't be trusted in small things, you can't be trusted in big things" (Luke 16:10-13). The deacon can't be in it for greedy gain—and not just money. Many people aren't motivated by getting money for themselves, but by popularity or power. The dishonest gain some seek isn't found primarily in the currency of cash, but in the ability to manipulate people. Now, there is something to be gained by serving as a faithful deacon. Verse 13 says as much. But a deacon doesn't lust after dishonest reward, but after the "treasures in heaven" (Matt. 6:20) that Jesus offers. In addition, I urge someone trustworthy to look at the generosity of the deacon candidate toward the church. Being unwilling to give to the church family often indicates trust, submission, and generosity problems in the heart—and we can't point people in the church to imitate this person.[12]

- **Deacons hold to the mystery of the faith with a clear conscience:** A deacon holds firmly in his mind and heart the truth of the gospel—the mystery of God's plan, from before the foundations of the Earth, to save and reconcile sinners to himself by the blood of his Son, Jesus (Eph. 1:4). The deacon *knows* the gospel. *Understands* the gospel. *Loves* and finds his *safety* and *identity* in the gospel. What's more, while a deacon doesn't have to be a competent teacher or public speaker, he should be able to verbalize the gospel. Even if communicated in a humble, imperfect way, the gospel should

12. *Unwilling* is completely different than *currently incapable*. For instance, the deacon candidate may have some extenuating financial circumstance (let's say an accident which has caused medical bills to squeeze every penny out of his pockets). If the heart of the deacon is to pay his debts and return to financial stability and be as generous as possible to his church, I think you can move forward with a clear conscience. There are a lot of "what if's" here, and an entire book couldn't cover them all adequately. Again, the Holy Spirit will guide each church whose leadership desires guidance.

be clear: Christ died for sinners! A deacon will hold to the gospel as a mystery that is only revealed in the divinely inspired Word of God. A deacon is a Bible person.

- **Deacons have their character tested as to blamelessness:** Over time and in community, the deacon is a person whose faith in God brings him to obey the Lord, not entering into sin to relieve anxiety or satisfy hungers. This person's allegiance and treasure is given to Jesus and his path for human flourishing in all areas of life, especially as it relates to money, sex, and power. For this reason, the godly character of a deacon must be tested.
- **The wife of a deacon should be like her husband and, in addition, not be a slanderer, must be sober-minded, and faithful:** I've been using a lot of the generic pronoun "he" when referring to deacons—we'll address the question of whether a woman can be a deacon soon. In any case, this trio of character traits definitely applies to the spouse of a deacon. Why would Paul require that a deacon's wife have good character?
- In the Bible, God says that when a man leaves his father and mother to be joined with a wife, the two become one flesh.
- As a Christian who holds to a biblical,

complementarian view of husband and wife roles, I'd argue that if a man is called by God to ministry then his wife (who is *one* with him) is part of that calling too.

- In my experience, when you get a man as a leader, you get his wife too. When the man and wife, as one, are godly, this is a blessing. If not, obviously, it's a real problem, to say the least.
- Think of how challenging it would be for a deacon to carry out his duties properly with an unclouded mind if his spouse was going around slandering and gossiping about people. The "single-tongued," trustworthy speech of the deacon would be undone by the work of his spouse's speech. Who would trust this deacon with sensitive knowledge when his spouse might divulge it in the form of gossip or slander?
- What would happen to the dignity and *gravitas* of a deacon if his spouse were acting foolishly?
- What a challenge it would be for the deacon who is trying to faithfully obey Jesus in everything while his spouse is unfaithful to the Lord!
- How difficult would it be for a deacon to hand

over time and energy to a calling and ministry that his wife is opposed to (for legitimate or illegitimate reasons)?

- **A deacon is the husband of one wife:** Many Christians will take this statement to mean that a deacon can never have been divorced and serve in the office of deacon. I, along with many other pastors and theologians, would disagree. This text indicates that the deacon is, in shorthand terms, a "one-woman man." It refers to the deacon's sexual purity. This doesn't just cover whether the deacon is guilty of adultery, but also fornication, consuming pornography, and any other forms of sexual perversion. The deacon is one who gladly enjoys sex within God's pure, good, beautiful design. If a deacon is unmarried, he mustn't engage in premarital sex. The Lord may see fit, in the future, to give this person a spouse, and premarital sex is a sin against his future beloved.
- **Deacons manage their children and their households well:** In this regard, deacons are to be like elders—demonstrating the ability to lead and serve their family in a way similar to how they'll have to lead and serve the church. Deacons are to lead by their Christian

example, not just at the church and as an agent of the church, but in the home. This shows us the central service a deacon performs for the church: a deacon is a lead servant, one who is a role model regardless of the amount of authority he carries in his service. We should be able to take any Christian and tell them to imitate a deacon, not just in serving, but in living too.

A Weighty Standard and Weighty Repentance

These character qualifications are a big deal. I'm sure many of you are probably reviewing your life and thinking, "Wow, am I even qualified to be a deacon?" I hope more people take the Lord's standard for leadership in ministry seriously. Too many pursue ministry leadership for the big three: sex, money, and power. Too many are wolves, looking to devour the sheep of the church. Too many young men want to "go into ministry" because it seems like a pretty sweet deal: it's air-conditioned work, you get to talk and have coffee with people, and you mainly just work on Sundays. So, if you're challenged by this, good for you. If you're working through a calling into ministry, especially, as a deacon, call on trusted Christians around you to help evaluate your character. If you're getting really worried about this list and whether you measure up, I hope to reassure you a bit.

The church doesn't need *perfect* leaders—we already

have one. His name's Jesus. What the church does need is repentant leaders, pursuing righteousness. If you've fallen in any of these ways and have demonstrated less-than-deacon-quality character, that might mean you should put your ministry pursuit on hold for a while—but only for as long as it takes for you and those around you to affirm that you've been walking in good character for an appropriate season. You may also need to recognize that though you have failed in some area—and you most certainly have at some point in the past—that doesn't mean you're disqualified forever. The questions to ask, with the help of your pastors and wise Christian counselors are:

- Have I truly repented (turned away from sin and turned toward Jesus in obedience) in these areas?
- Have I been walking with a consistent level of victory and obedience here?
- Am I, like an elder, living a life that's "above reproach?"[13]
- Are other Christians able to affirm that I have

13. 1 Tim. 3:2. The qualifications for an elder aren't the same as those of a deacon, but they are closely related, both being formal offices in the church. It seems right that a deacon should share the conviction to live a godly life, above reproach. A heart of repentance is so vital here, since the call isn't to be a functionally perfect person, but a person functionally repenting as they pursue Christ's perfection. Repentance will mean that the deacon's desire is to live "above reproach," knowing that they're not *beyond* reproach. When convicted of sin, a deacon's ready to confess and repent.

the godly character of a deacon?

I can't stress this enough: Pastors, do right by the church and the candidate by performing the due diligence of your office to guard the church from unqualified leaders and guard those leaders from entering into an office they aren't prepared for. You don't have to find people with *perfect* character—just people characterized by a lifestyle of repentant obedience.

What about Competency?

Of course, deacons *do* have to do stuff. What kind of skills or abilities are required of a deacon? The Bible is largely silent, except for the job description of a deacon—they have to be good at serving the church. Whatever competencies you require in a deacon, they should be related to the service a deacon performs. That's why my church doesn't require that deacons be able to preach—that's a competency requirement for elders, not deacons. We wouldn't require a quarterback to be able to kick the field goals, would we? We wouldn't require a pitcher to be competent to swing a baseball bat, right? *Right, American League? Right?*

We'll cover specific categories of competency for deacons in chapter four. For now, we'll simply state that the capacity the deacon's going to serve in will determine the competencies that are required. The deacon has to be able to actually serve the church in his area of ministry.

So . . . Female Deacons. Yes or No?

You knew it was coming—or, some of you were just hoping it would come up: Should churches install women as deacons? I have a simple answer. Are you ready? *Whatever God says, we'll do.* Okay, I admit, that's kind of a cop-out. So, let's try to answer that question in a little more detail.

What Does the Bible Say?

Of course, we have to ask that question. No surprise there. Any book on the church office of deacon should submit to the authority of the Bible first. In this case, the Bible offers no explicit guidance on the matter. At first glance, some may point to Romans 16, where Phoebe, a woman in the church at Cenchrea, is referred to as a servant (*diakonos*). Well, that settles it! Woman. *Diakonos.* Next topic!

Not so fast, my friend. We've already established that the New Testament Scriptures use the term *diakonos* a lot, and it's mostly used in the general sense, not referring to the *office* of deacon. There's not enough in that text to conclusively determine that, yes, Phoebe is a Christian woman, filling the formal office of deacon in the church. We're going to have to look at the broader scope of the Scriptures, engaging biblical gender roles in the church.

Before we move forward, let's remember this book is about deacons, not one on gender roles in the church.

My recommended resource for biblical views on gender is John Piper and Wayne Grudem's *Recovering Biblical Manhood and Womanhood: A Response to Evangelical Feminism*. Their helpful teaching in the matter has led me to conclude that the church is most healthy and robust when Christian women are most free to walk in the spiritual gifts and power God grants, in every way that God says they should. No door to ministry should be closed to a godly woman—no door, excepting the one that God's Word closes. Otherwise, a qualified, godly Christian woman should be free and *encouraged* to serve the church and empower the leaders, being rewarded with honor and respect for her faithfulness.

I stand firm on the position that the office of elder has been reserved, by God, for men—and it hasn't got anything to do with men being "better," "stronger," "smarter," or "less emotional." I stand firm because I know I can stand on whatever God says, even if it's challenging to my sensibilities or hard to understand. I also, however, stand *humbly* on this doctrine. I don't have the authority to structure the church and determine the roles. In some ways, it's mysterious to me why men, who are in essence no better and no worse than women, were selected to be candidates for the pastorate. I have known wise, mature, stable, gifted, godly women who I admire and constantly think, "Sheesh. That's someone I need to imitate!" not in their femininity (which is *beautiful* and *precious*!), but in their godly character and ability. So, you won't get any machoistic chest-pounding from me on how *obviously sensible* it is for God to reserve the pastorate for men and not women. I'm humbled that the Lord would call me to be an elder to many people—women included—who are smarter or more skilled than I am in a variety of areas.

The Broader Scope of Scripture

The only office in the church that is closed to women is that of elder. There's something particularly unique about this office in that women aren't called to do the authoritative leading and preaching as elders over the church body (1 Tim. 2:11-14). Keep in mind that this restriction is a bit narrower in scope than many traditional churches have treated it.

Women in the Bible have always been loved and called by God to do great, significant, powerful things. Women are to learn the Scriptures, disciple people, and serve in many other ways. The wisdom, grace, and steadiness of godly women demonstrates that God never intended for women to be second-class citizens in his kingdom:

- Esther found herself thrust into the precarious position of being the wife of a pagan king. She was surrounded by enemies seeking to destroy her people. With shrewdness and political savvy, she spoke wisdom powerfully to her king, rescuing her people and seeing the enemy defeated.

- Ruth, widowed and far from home, bound herself to her mother-in-law Naomi, as well as to Naomi's God, *Jehovah*. She was committed, faithful, generous, and extremely hard-working. With dignity and modesty, she made her qualities apparent to Boaz, who saw not just her beauty, but her good character. Intelligent and capable, she became a noble wife and manager, as well as the great-grandmother of King David.
- We shouldn't simply credit Mary for giving birth to Jesus—this woman magnified and worshiped the Lord in the midst of social disgrace as an unwed pregnant woman. Facing the possibility of her fiancé, Joseph, leaving her in public shame, and probably worried about being executed, she kept her unborn son healthy and alive. If that's not enough, I doubt any of us would want the stressful job of being the earthly mom of the Messiah. How confident would you be that something toddler-Jesus did was a spanking offense? Would you be strong enough to endure watching your beloved son be lied about, rejected, beaten, mocked, abandoned by his best friends, and murdered brutally on a Roman cross? Mary would have to be, if

nothing else, a strong, faithful woman. (And she was, as we later learn that she was among the redeemed believers of Christ!)

- Priscilla, the wife of Aquila, was of great help in discipling young Apollos. This gifted preacher needed his theology straightened out and Priscilla teamed with her husband to spend a lot of time with him. This was in addition to her faithful church-planting efforts as a member of Paul's core team in Corinth and Ephesus.
- Finally, Paul reminded Timothy of the fruitful teaching work that his grandma, Lois, and his mom, Eunice, did for him. Timothy's "sincere faith," Paul says, "dwelt first in your grandmother . . . and your mother." The Bible has, for 2,000 years, honored these women by name for their service in teaching and discipling Timothy, the future pastor.

These examples clearly bear witness to the wide scope of ministry performed by women in the Scriptures. No, none of these women are identified as Christians serving in the formal office of deacon, but they absolutely serve God's people influentially and with distinction! This should lead us to believe that there's little-to-no reason to restrict women from the diaconate. While the office of elder is closed to women, it seems little else is.

We can even look to the historical views of church fathers—which should carry some weight with us, but of course, not nearly as much as the Scriptures. The early church father John Chrysostom read 1 Timothy 3:11 as referring to women who hold the rank of deaconess.[14] The Greek term employed by Paul is *gunaikas*, seeming to indicate that this references women deacons. Chrysostom didn't seem to see a problem with women as deacons. I don't think we should, either.[15]

When we compare the qualifications for eldership in 1 Timothy 3:1-7 with those of the deacon in 3:8-12, we see there aren't any qualifications for women to be elders. But there are qualifications for women as deacons, if we're interpreting the Scriptures as plainly as possible and respecting the early church's views of the matter. It's not required for deacons to be employed in the authoritative teaching and leadership of the church, though some deacons will teach and lead. Depending on the ministry role of the woman deacon and the scope of leadership authority the particular ministry commands, she can be called on to teach and disciple and wield influence in the church with a clear conscience.

---

14. Thomas C. Oden, *Classic Christianity: A Systematic Theology*.

15. Restoration City Church has informally elected to call men and women serving in this office as *deacons*, and not differentiating the genders with the added title *deaconess*. No big reason, other than it's a funny word and gets trippy to spell it and say it. If you want to use it, have at it!

Indeed, it's Paul (the guy who established the gender limitations of the pastorate to men) who praises Phoebe, a deacon in the church of Cenchreae. Some theologians have even speculated that it was Phoebe who served as courier of the Roman Epistle for Paul. That would have been be a pretty important service role.

In short, it seems that we shouldn't stand in the way of *any* Christian who has:

- Demonstrated godly character over time and in community
- Demonstrated evidence of submission to the leadership of the pastors of their local church
- Demonstrated the necessary competency the office requires

If a Christian satisfies these requirements, then we have a reliable deacon candidate on our hands—because that's who a deacon is.

Chapter 4

What Do Deacons Do?

Now in these days when the disciples were increasing in number, a complaint by the Hellenists arose against the Hebrews because their widows were being neglected in the daily distribution. And the twelve summoned the full number of the disciples and said, "It is not right that we should give up preaching the word of God to serve tables. Therefore, brothers, pick out from among you seven men of good repute, full of the Spirit and of wisdom, whom we will appoint to this duty."

—Acts 6:1-3

What Do Deacons Do?

Well, duh. They serve. End of chapter four. Best chapter ever, right? Your pastor or ministry leader told you to read this book. Four chapters down, two more to go. Phew!

Not so fast, kemosabe. There's plenty more to say. Stick with me. Let's talk about what deacons *actually* do.

Deacons Serve . . . but Whom Do They Serve?

On Mars Hill in Athens, the Apostle Paul got into an epic rap battle with a bunch of Greek philosophers (Acts 17:16-31). He spent a few days touring the city, studying the Athenians and their religions. He found a statue dedicated to some "unknown god." This was the Athenians' religious insurance policy against forgetting some god and being punished for failing to worship it out of ignorance.

To these philosophers, Paul said, "Hey! You kind of get it! There *is* a god you don't know. I'm here to tell you about him." Paul preached, telling them that his God isn't a statue to offer sacrifices to, doesn't live in some temple, and doesn't need humans to bring him food or drink or sacrifices. In fact, this God, Jesus, is the one who brings mankind life!

If we hear Paul rightly, we understand that deacons don't serve God—at least, not in a way that God depends on. If your church doesn't have deacons, or is low on people serving, it's not like God's plans are thwarted and he's wringing his hands in worry. God's the one who accomplishes his will. He's the one who gives life. He's the one from whom all matter, energy, and truth come from.

Now, I could get into big trouble for using that passage to say, "Deacons don't serve God," and then moving on. I'm not going to do that. Let's take a look at Romans 12:11. The same Paul who said that God isn't served by human hands wrote to the church in Rome and told them: "Serve the Lord." What gives? Do deacons serve the Lord, or not? Yes and no.

God's people do serve the Lord, but not in the way that pagans have historically understood serving a deity. I can't take a lot of time to do a historical examination of world religions, so let me just do a gross generalization. In pagan religions, people have worshiped graven images (statues of metal or wood), believing that they need to bring food, water, and sacrifices to their "god" to sustain his work and lordship over them. These pagan gods would need the service of their people, otherwise they would no longer be able to cover them with their power and good fortune. Basically, the thinking went, *If we don't do something for our god, he can't do something for us.*

We who have heard and received the gospel know this isn't how our God works. The gospel says that, before we could ever do anything for God, he did everything for us that we need:

- **Romans 5:6**—"For while we were still weak,

at the right time Christ died for the ungodly."

- **Romans 5:8**—"But God shows his love for us in that while we were still sinners, Christ died for us."
- **Ephesians 2:4,5**—"But God, being rich in mercy, because of the great love with which he loved us, even when we were dead in our trespasses, made us alive together with Christ."
- **Ephesians 2:8, 9**—"For by grace you have been saved through faith. And this is not your own doing; it is the gift of God, not a result of works, so that no one may boast."

I started this book with the gospel, which informs us why Jesus designed his church with deacons in mind. Deacons serve because Jesus serves. We don't serve God to get good things from God; we serve God because we've already received good things from God. Deacons aren't the expression of service to God in a way that he needs, but an expression of how we have needed God to serve us!

I said earlier that deacons do serve the Lord, but in what way? Let's go back to Romans 12. Look at the verses surrounding the command in verse 11 to "serve the Lord."

> For by the grace given to me I say to everyone among you not to think of himself more highly than he ought to think, but to think with sober judgment, each according to the measure of faith that God has assigned. *For as in one body*

we have many members, and the members do not all have the same function, so we, though many, are one body in Christ, and individually members *one of another*. Having gifts that differ according to the grace given to us, *let us use them*: if prophecy, in proportion to our faith; *if service, in our serving*; the one who teaches, in his teaching; the one who exhorts, in his exhortation; the one who contributes, in generosity; the one who leads, with zeal; the one who does acts of mercy, with cheerfulness. Let love be genuine. Abhor what is evil; hold fast to what is good. *Love one another with brotherly affection. Outdo one another in showing honor.* Do not be slothful in zeal, be fervent in spirit, *serve the Lord*. Rejoice in hope, be patient in tribulation, be constant in prayer. *Contribute to the needs of the saints and seek to show hospitality.* Bless those who persecute you; bless and do not curse them. Rejoice with those who rejoice, weep with those who weep. Live in harmony with one another. Do not be haughty, but associate with the lowly. Never be wise in your own sight. Repay no one evil for evil, but give thought to do what is honorable in the sight of all. *If possible, so far as it depends on you, live peaceably with all.*

—Rom. 12:3-18 (emphasis added)

What was Paul primarily talking about in that passage? He was talking about how Christians should relate to one another as God's people. In the context of being Christians, in the church and as the church on mission, Paul instructed them (and us) on how to love one another the way God has loved us. Included in his instruction is the command to "serve the Lord."

Deacons serve the Lord by serving God's people. In my own life, those who demonstrate the most love for me are those who love my family. What did Jesus tell Peter after he asked Peter if he loved him? "Feed my sheep" (John 21:17). In fact, Jesus repeated it three times. Jesus said of the Final Judgment:

> Come, you who are blessed by my Father, inherit the kingdom prepared for you from the foundation of the world. For I was hungry and you gave me food, I was thirsty and you gave me drink, I was a stranger and you welcomed me, I was naked and you clothed me, I was sick and you visited me, I was in prison and you came to me.
>
> —Matt. 25:34-36

The redeemed saints will stand amazed and bewildered, thinking, *I don't remember ever having done that for you, Jesus. In fact, I lived about 2,000 years after you lived.* And Jesus will answer, "Truly, I say to you, as you did it to one of the least of these, my brothers, you did it to me." What does a deacon do? Jesus says a deacon serves God by serving God's people.

How Do Deacons Serve?

In the early church (Acts 6), church life appeared pretty similar to what it's like today. But in some ways, it was also pretty different. The need for deacons arose because the church had two primary ministries—the ministry of preaching and teaching, and the ministry of distributing food to the needy. The pastors needed to focus on prayer, preaching, and leadership, so deacons were appointed to handle some of the more practical aspects of serving.

In many churches today, there's so many more things to do and get done. Things like handling finances, administration, building management, outreach, marketing, musical worship, and a host of other things.[16] So many things! Deacons are of vital importance in our churches today, just as they were 2,000 years ago.

I started planting a church in 2012. In the early days, service opportunities were slim because we had about fourteen people, no building, and we just met on Friday evenings for prayer, preaching, and singing. (We didn't even have a sound system, guitar player, or words on a

---

16. By the way, if your church is feeling overwhelmed by all these things to do, you've got to read Tim Chester and Steve Timmis's book *Total Church* (Crossway, 2008).

screen—just a godly woman who stood up front and coaxed us into singing old hymns a capella!) Service to the church mainly consisted of pulling couches together in the church lobby we met in, lighting some candles, and printing out the hymn sheets—and I did all of that because I didn't have a whole lot else to do.

As the church grew, however, the need for faithful servants who would take responsibility for the church grew also. Our church already had an elder (me). After about a year, we were in need of deacons to start handling administrative tasks and other ministry work.

What Deacons Do and Don't Do for the Church

The authoritative, biblically-driven leadership of the church comes from our Lead Shepherd, Jesus, through his Word, and then through his under-shepherds, the pastors. In addition, we can confidently say, from Acts 6 and elsewhere, that the preaching and governing of the church is restricted to the elders. There are many churches today that are governed by a body of people called a "deacon board." Typically, these boards consist of non-elders who serve the church as deacons, governing in a manner that is, according to the Scriptures, outside of the purview of a deacon. I disagree with and discourage this form of government, not because it's simply a different governing style than the one I adhere to, but because it doesn't reflect the one the Bible sets forth.

With that said, just about everything else the church needs done can be the work of a deacon. Let's consider the various ministries Paul identifies in Romans 12 as a way to get at some of the specific ways a deacon might serve the church:

- **Prophecy (v. 6):** Truth-telling and specific instruction from the Lord. This is a tricky one. I'm not really into people running around telling others, "I'm a prophet! Listen to me! I have a word from the Lord!" It seems the office of prophet ended with Jesus (who's the perfect, true prophet). That said, it seems that some hear especially well from the Holy Spirit and are gifted with clarity and power in speaking God's truth into particular situations. With any prophetic, "special" word from God that someone has to offer us, we must follow the apostle John's instructions from 1 John 4:1-6 to "test the spirits" against the Word of God.
- **Serving (v. 7):** This includes a wide range of possible activities. Building, cleaning, serving coffee, arranging chairs, rocking babies in the nursery, bringing food to the sick and elderly, printing bulletins, mowing lawns, and the list goes on. Many will call this area of ministry "helps." Some people are just good at helping—they know what needs to be done

right away and they always seem to be one step ahead of other people, prepared to do what's needed, whether gathering tools, equipment, food, etc. These tireless folks, like David, a deacon in my church, are a huge blessing to the church! These are reliable, indispensable people. Think in terms of outreach, building maintenance, host team, and anything else that needs capable workers.

- **Teaching (v. 7):** Those deacons with the gift of teaching may find opportunities to teach others in the church. Under the authority of the elders, a deacon might teach a Bible study, kids' ministry class, or membership class. Should a deacon preach? I think not, as that's a ministry role reserved for elders. How can you tell the difference between preaching and teaching? A lot of people can't. This isn't a book on preaching, but my nutshell version is that preaching is louder and sweatier. It's not merely instructive, but authoritative in that it carries the weight of the pastorate. Teaching is primarily for instructional formation—it can hold the authority of leadership (like a kids' ministry teacher instructing children), but it doesn't hold the church-wide authority of preaching. These teaching deacons may also turn out to be good counselors.

- **Exhortation (v. 8):** Encouragement! "Jesus loves you! The Father delights in you! You have the Holy Spirit in you! Trust in God's Word—it's power! Rise to your feet! Lace up your boots! Get to work! You can obey the Lord, and however it turns out, you're valued and approved of in Christ!" The church needs deacons who use these kinds of words to put steel in our spines and fire in our bellies. We also need deacons who use words of kindness, empathy, and sympathy. People who encourage with hugs and tears and gifts of food. These deacons are often good on social media, reaching and encouraging large numbers of God's people. These, too, can be good counselors.
- **Contribution (v. 8):** There are some deacons who are powerfully righteous and wise with money. Sometimes, God enables someone to be good at making the dollars show up. Sometimes, God enables someone (with either a lot of money or very little money of their own) to give sacrificially—think Elijah and the woman to whom God kept miraculously giving oil in jars. The church needs deacons who are righteous and trustworthy with their own finances and those of the church. These

folks are helpful as examples to the rest of the church in giving and are often gifted in managing finances in the church (the team that counts the offering, etc).

- **Leadership (v. 8):** Some deacons are really good managers and leaders. They know how to get people on the bus and in the right seats. They take responsibility for the spiritual growth and the ministry work of others. A lot of other gifts (exhortation, helps, teaching) will often show up in this sort of deacon as they lead church members. This sort of deacon will definitely lead by example—people can imitate this deacon as he or she imitates Jesus.
- **Acts of Mercy (v. 8):** When I try to work in this way, I feel like Sheldon Cooper, awkwardly patting someone's shoulder and muttering, "there, there."[17] But, when one of the women at my church (Meghan) does it, it's natural and beautiful. If I visit you in sickness, you'll probably react with "Meh." When Meghan shows up to hug you and pray for you, there's tears and sweetness and an overwhelming sense of God's mercy. This sort of deacon shows kindness to those who are

17. Uber-nerd Sheldon Cooper, played by actor Jim Parsons on *The Big Bang Theory*.

> most fragile and weak. They pour out God's mercy on his lost, sick sheep because they share Jesus's brokenheartedness for his "little ones." A deacon who serves with acts of mercy is like a refreshing drink of cold water in the middle of the desert.

When deacons are busy *deaconing*, they end up leading and encouraging all the saints to serve. I'll never forget the moment in the HBO series *Band of Brothers* when Lieutenant Dick Winters, under a hail of fire coming in from the town of Carentan, stands up, rips his helmet off, and starts shouting at his cowering brothers to "Move forward!" Deacons are the ones who stand up, ready for the challenge, urging on their brothers and sisters in Christ to move forward as they lead the way.

Under Authority

In cases where deacons serve the church in management or leadership (i.e., wielding influence), they do so, as all deacons do, under the authority of the elders. This is why the godly character of a deacon must be considered before his skill. The ability for an influential, gifted deacon to serve the church is amazing. So is his or her ability to hurt the church. At Restoration City Church, we strive to install leaders who have shown that they can trust and submit to the pastoral leadership of the church. If someone wants to be in authority, they need to demonstrate that they can do well under authority.

Rather than forming a committee of deacons, run by deacons, we have (at my church) elected to organize the *diaconate* by ministry, under the leadership of an elder. This way elders can focus on training and reviewing the work of their deacons, rather than doing the work for the deacons and micromanaging them.

Communication between elders and deacons is paramount. When elders consider making larger, sweeping, ministry-wide decisions, they'll lead best when they discuss and seek ground-level wisdom from the people who are primarily doing the work—the deacons. One of the most frustrating things for a deacon who's trying to faithfully serve the church is an out-of-leftfield decision coming down from the elders, without any opportunity to offer input or any kind of heads-up. Leading deacons should be invited as often as possible to lend a voice to the deliberations of the elders—it's a stupid lieutenant who doesn't listen to the experienced wisdom and ground-level info of his sergeants. The Bible has something to say to both elders and deacons in this case: "Without counsel, plans fail, but with many advisers they succeed" (Prov. 15:22).

The general attitude we want our deacons to have when being led by their elders is, "I'm ready to say 'yes' to whatever you tell me to do. But before I go about making it happen, would you please let me tell you my reservations and suggestions?" The general attitude of our elders should be, "I need to know you trust me and will submit to me, but I want you to know I'm listening and taking your wisdom and advice seriously—I'm not above learning from you and having my mind changed."

In the healthiest version of this dynamic, elders should trust their wise deacons to prayerfully and righteously serve the church. Elders should be on guard of exercising too much oversight. This isn't to say elders shouldn't exercise *any* oversight—but, if the elders are actually leading their deacons and communicating, they'll have all the oversight they need on how the ministry is going.

Deacons, too, should trust their leaders—trusting that the elders trust them. When the deacons at Restoration City Church wonder if they should ask for counsel or permission before making a big service decision, they almost always check in. If you can keep communication effective and streamlined, good decisions can get made in good time because of trust.

If we can recognize that the office of deacon isn't a "second-class" office in the church, but serves a vital role in the church's ministry, then our deacons are set up to succeed in their service—their work for God's people will become a "manifestation of the Spirit for the common good" (1 Cor. 12:7), bringing unity to the church. When the *lead servant* deacons have *servant-leader* elders, this whole church thing works pretty well for everyone.[18]

In his book, *Sticky Teams,* Larry Osborne identifies a sort of sweet spot where elders make very few ground-level ministry calls, give some permissions, and mostly review and redirect ministry that's already happening. Again, this will take a lot of work—ensuring that the character of both elders and deacons is godly,[19] making sure deacons are serving in the areas they should, and building a healthy church leadership team.[20]

Speaking of Authority . . .

Once a church has more than one deacon in place, someone's going to want to know who's the boss of the other guy. We're built and wired to demand an understanding of what authority structure we're working

---

18. When Jesus says that the leader should become one who serves, he doesn't mean that elders—who don't primarily serve in material work, but in leadership and preaching—are supposed to spend their time taking out the garbage, cleaning toilets, and mowing widows' lawns. What he *does* mean is that the elder should have a lowliness and humility of heart that is shared with deacons.

19. When we consider the calling and character of an elder candidate, we get really serious. Because the Bible tells church members to obey their pastors (Heb. 13:17), we want to make sure that the pastors they have are men worthy of being obeyed.

20. Seriously, on the topic of a healthy church leadership, you need to read both Osborne's *Sticky Teams* (Zondervan, 2010) and Patrick Lencioni's *The Advantage* (Josey-Bass, 2012).

with. Everyone knows that while the teacher runs the classroom, there are other leaders on the playground: some kids are in charge and other kids listen. While the Bible lays out a clear structure of authority in the church—the elders authoritatively govern and lead the church and the deacons submit by carrying out their role as lead servants in ministry—some deacons will inevitably get curious about how their ministry positions measure up against other deacons.

Of first importance is to see that each deacon tests and purifies his or her heart when this question comes up. Pride, arrogance, and power-seeking for personal benefit have no place in the *diaconate*. If mutual submission is hard, that deacon might need some counsel and repentance.[21] Nevertheless, the elders should try to establish and clearly communicate the economic structure of the diaconate to avoid confusion—without clear structures in place, you could have deacons creating their own factions that war with other factions, and nobody wants to have to deal with that kind of anarchy.

In the process of researching the *diaconate* and talking out these ideas with other pastors, questions like this have come up several times: Won't a deacon who's in charge of

---

21. Mutual, or peer, submission, as opposed to submission to elders. We're speaking in purely economical terms here, and not in ontological terms (governmental hierarchy, rather than your value as a person).

significant, larger ministries or teams feel like his office is cheapened or watered down if someone who coordinates three others to serve meals to the homeless is also called a deacon? The worry is that you might dilute the apparent weight of the office if you call both roles the same classifying title. The answer to the question, of course, is no. Not if our deacons are humbly unconcerned with the personal glory or praise of the office.

In the army, you have a class of soldier called *officer*. A lieutenant is an officer, and a colonel is an officer. While the second lieutenant is in charge of up to around forty people, the colonel is responsible for three to four thousand! Any colonel who gets his little silver eagle pins bothered by the fact that he and the lieutenant are both referred to as officers has a problem. They both lead and serve their country. They both have the same calling, but vastly different job descriptions and titles. The term "officer," regardless of which rank we're talking about, still carries the nobility of its calling. And that's just about as far as I want to take this military analogy for deacons. This is Christ's bride, after all, not the U.S. Army.

So, too, with deacons. That's probably all we should say about it, too. The more we discuss it, the more we invite the "But, what abouts" that get us bogged down in who should be more important than whom, and then the Holy Spirit will have to come in and rebuke us with that verse he wrote, saying, "The last shall be first and the first shall be last" (Matt. 20:16).

A Godly Division of Labor

When elders are doing what only elders should do, and when deacons are doing all that deacons should do, the church is set up to flourish. The saints are served and led to serve. Jesus is honored. The gospel is put on full display.

There are a variety of staff positions in the church that are non-elder roles. I believe that anyone the church can call upon to serve in a staff capacity should be of proven, godly character, committed to Jesus and the church, submissive to the elders, and faithful to serve—that's a deacon. But, what about church members who should be deacons but don't fit a particular category or position in the church? Like the guy who serves coffee at the host team table? Or the lady who serves the children's ministry, scheduling the volunteers every month and hosing down all the toys with Lysol every Sunday afternoon? They don't really have a "job title." Should they be deacons?

Sure. Why not? At my church (and in many others), this sort of deacon is considered an at-large deacon. When someone is installed into the formal office of deacon, they don't automatically get a promotion into more responsibility or authority. The lady who manages the choir or worship team's inventory might be serving in the fullness of her capacity—to install her as a deacon and then to expect her to lead the choir or team might be beyond her calling, and that would crush her and damage the team.

So, we may have uncategorized at-large deacons who serve the church.[22] Their primary work, in whatever ministry they serve, is to be an imitation-worthy Christian. So, when you have someone new to the host team, pair him up with the coffee-pouring deacon. They'll be in good hands with this good example. If you have someone who needs a mature influence in her life, have her serve with the deacon who brings meals to the elderly each week. The idea here is that the deacon is a called church member of proven godly character who faithfully serves the church.

Command Authority versus Influence Authority

It might be profitable for us to consider the varied sorts of deacons in terms of what kind of authority they are called to wield. It seems that some deacon-leaders serve with what we can call *command authority* and others serve with *influence authority.* Remember, we're calling our churches to imitate our deacons as they imitate Christ, which implies some sort of leadership quality.

A deacon who wields command authority is someone who is handed a specific scope of responsibility to tell

22. Some churches might elect not to have "at-large" deacons. That's fine, too. It may be seen as too vague a role for some structures. Others might decide to employ the office of "at-large deacon" as a training role—say, a role in which the individual is not wielding much influence or authority, but is being trained or groomed for just such a future appointment.

others what must be done, how it must be done, and when it must be done. The deacon who leads my church's host team is charged with wielding command authority over his volunteers. It's his say on what sort of coffee we're serving, what rooms need to be vacuumed, who's going to clean the mirrors in the bathroom, and so on. His volunteers are expected to trust him and do as he instructs. Note that his command authority doesn't go beyond the host team, and his authority is given to him by Jesus, the Bible, and his pastors.

Deacons who have command authority will normally be over a ministry team of some sort, or possibly serve in a staff capacity. At-large deacons really don't fall into this category of authority. Because, as we'll see in a moment, command authority is so much weightier than influence authority, the character of these deacons and their ability to submit themselves to the authority of their elders really has to be tested thoroughly.

Influence authority is generally more subtle. In every church (and in any organization) there are people who don't have a job title, office, or appointed position. They might not be acknowledged as having any specific role, but the elders can see that the people around them—the people in their sphere of influence—are listening and influenced by them. Often, these influencers leverage this influence authority. Sadly, they too often don't. So many times, churches are damaged and divided by people with influence authority who are angry they aren't on staff, are frustrated that their opinions aren't being considered enough, or just want to assert their own values or plans.

Deacons at-large tend to operate from this "influence authority" position. They really aren't in a position to tell anyone what to do, but then again, they don't have to. People trust them, like them, and want to be like them. This is why a deacon who "just" pours coffee or "just" works in the tech booth can still rightly be considered a leader—he or she is capable of influencing others for the good of the church and its mission. This influence carries similar if not the same weight of simple authority.

We shouldn't draw too much distinction between these two types of authority, either. For instance, if a deacon is to be given some sort of command authority, he or she should have already demonstrated a natural gift for leadership by demonstrating influence authority.

Clarity of Calling

Every deacon should have a clear understanding of how he or she is serving the church. Deacons might serve in a variety of ways, but they need to know what they do, how to do it (because they're being trained and led by elders, right?), and why they do it. Later on, I'll share with you Restoration City Church's protocol for identifying, qualifying, and training deacons. For now, let's consider how deacon candidates are first called to be deacons.

Every deacon does something, accomplishes something, and strives in some specific work of the church. We want them to know where and how God wants them to serve.

My Testimony of Being Called

I remember when I first believed I was being called to pastor. It was the pits. It was terribly confusing and I was filled with a lot of anxiety. Thankfully, I had some excellent friends and pastors listening to me, praying for me, and doing their best to help me discern my calling. So to say working through my calling was terrible isn't to say anything negative about them. But I do mean to critique the modern church's usual way of working through a person's calling. We need to be able to offer better help to those seeking to understand a call from God.

What we refer to as a "calling" is simply a unique, spiritual beckoning from God to do or be a particular thing. It comes from the Latin term *voca,* from which we get the word "vocalization." We often call what someone does for a living their "vocation"—the one doing the "vocalizing" is God, and he's speaking to a Christian. In a general way, we've already established that all Christians are called to be priests and ministers. We're all called to serve the church as *diakonos*, in the general sense of that word. But answering questions like: "Am I called to be a pastor? A deacon? To move to Oklahoma and start a vinyl siding business? To marry my sweetheart?" Those can be really tough questions to answer.

Too often, what we pastors think when someone says, "Pastor, I think I'm called to the ministry!" is:

- Is this person a Christian?
- Are they nice?
- Do they have skill?
- Do I like them?
- Do they think like I do?

Well, gosh. If they have the warm fuzzies, and I have the warm fuzzies, and they're a good Christian . . . I guess they're called! Sometimes, we get it right. Often, we get it wrong. I don't want to affirm anyone's calling that isn't actually called. I also don't want to stand in the way of someone I might not like or I might disagree with if God really is calling them! What do we do? How do we help?

First, I want to mention, again, Dave Harvey's excellent book *Am I Called?* It's so helpful! In addition, I offer the following thoughts to help you and those you lead (deacon candidates!) Through the process of discerning a potential calling to a particular ministry, office, or role.

Is This Calling Christ-Centered?

Colossians 3 and 1 Corinthians 10 both say that, if you're going to do something, it must be done for the Lord and for the purpose of glorifying him. If you want to know if God is calling you to some ministry, career, or other assignment, it's going to have to be a *godly* calling—that is, it'll agree with God's design for humanity as well as with his commands. It must bring Jesus honor and glory in your obedience to his Word. God won't call you to leave your wife to be with your secretary, and he's not going to call anyone to be a stripper or heroin dealer. He does, however, call people to things that are in line with his righteousness.

Do You Have the Character for This Calling?

Some things require a particular kind of person, and we're not talking skills or talents (at the moment). Some careers or pursuits require bravery and toughness, while others require tenderness and patience. In 1 Timothy 3 and Titus 1, God lists the character qualities of a pastor—if God's calling a man to be a pastor, then the man will already demonstrate this kind of character. Again, this isn't about what you can do. It's about what kind of person you are. So, what do you think God's calling you to be and do? What sort of character traits are necessary for it, and are you that kind of person? Is your character confirmed by others? Don't just take your own opinion of yourself and run with it. We tend to either overestimate or underestimate who we are. Character is revealed over time and in community. So, find out if the leaders over you can confirm that you have the necessary character for the calling in question. What do your peers think? What about those you already lead? In other words, seek honest input from others before assuming you're called into something.

Do You Have the Competency for This Calling?

Sometimes, there's a particular set of skills that a calling requires. You might know all of the stats for the team, personally be close friends with the players, have a terrific heart, love the game, and be really committed, but if you can't actually throw, you're not called to pitch. One of the things the Bible says about the calling to the pastorate (1 Tim. 3) is that a man has to be able to preach and teach the Word. If you can't, your calling to be a pastor is in serious question. (Of course, none of us starts off as a masterful preacher or teacher, but the gifting and ability to improve should be there.) What is it you think God wants you to do? What kind of skills or gifts are required for the task?

Do You Have the Conviction for This Calling?

Some call it passion, others call it unction. I'll call it conviction, since every item on this list starts with "c." Do you have a deep-seated passion, born from either enthusiasm or brokenheartedness, to strive and stick with this calling, whether it goes well for you or not? Is it rooted firmly in the soil of your soul that you must do this and see it through? Would quitting halfway through or finding something easier or more fun be out of the question? Satan tempts Jesus (Matt. 4) away from his Father's calling by offering Jesus earthly rewards: power and kingdoms and a life where he doesn't have to die for his enemies. Jesus rejected it, staying committed to a difficult ministry that would end with him dying on a Roman cross—and we're thankful (and saved!) Because Jesus's conviction held true. Because of Paul's conviction that he was called to pastor and plant churches, he "beats his body into submission" every morning (1 Cor. 9:27). In the womb, John the Baptizer was "filled with the Holy Spirit," which developed into a conviction that he needed to faithfully complete his God-given mission. Do you have that kind of conviction, believing that you must obey in the way God seems to be calling you?

Do You Have the Commitment to Keep Going in a Particular Calling?

Closely related to conviction is the question of whether you have the commitment it takes to stick with the difficulties associated with following God's call. If God is calling you to buy a house, will you remain committed and faithful to paying the mortgage each month and spending the necessary upkeep money? As the people you lead or serve betray you, leave you, or simply fail you, will you stick with them even though you feel all alone and unappreciated? In his grace, Jesus was committed to Judas's good all the way to the end. Though he knew the evil Judas intended to do, Jesus still invited him to the Last Supper, still broke bread with him, and still washed his betrayer's feet (John 13-14). Will you stick with your calling when the going gets tough?

Do You Have Chemistry with Others Who Are Involved?

Many times, God calls us to work with a team or group of people. This doesn't necessarily mean you have to be best buddies with everyone involved, but you should ask yourself if you simply like the others well enough to spend the required time together that the calling would require. Is it a culture of mutual respect and trust? At Restoration City Church, if we want to hire a pastor, and find a man who's talented, has great character, and seems passionate, but just doesn't fit with the personalities of our staff and members, he's not called to be a pastor with us (but probably is called to another church!).

Awakening Aspiration

I once heard a brilliant preaching and teaching pastor say, "Train the called, don't call the trained." That's great counsel; it expresses, in brief, what I've urged you to consider: character and calling are more important than mere competency. Don't just consider skilled people as deacon material. God sometimes uses us to initiate someone's calling by awakening their aspirations and helping them see things in themselves they were unaware of.

For instance, in Acts 6, the elders tell the church body to "appoint," or choose from among them, the men who would become deacons. That doesn't seem to be a prescription for how every church is to install deacons, but instead, descriptive of what they had to do at the time. There may be godly people with good character and service skills in your church who haven't yet expressed a desire to serve as deacons. While I'd recommend against just appointing them ("Duck, duck, *deacon!* Hey, guess what, Carl?! You're a deacon! Have fun and good luck!"), it's often a good leader who sees potential in those he leads; it's a good leader whom God often uses to awaken aspiration in others.

I won't forget what the Lord did for me through Beau, the pastor of a larger church in my community. When I was in high school, he was my youth pastor. My family was unexpectedly tied up one evening after my youth group met, and I got a ride home from Beau. He'd never been a big talker, and I had sometimes wondered if he even liked me. Regardless, he'd been watching me, paying attention.

On the way home, Beau asked, nonchalantly, "What are you going to do when you get out of high school, Matt?" I'm sure I muttered something moronic and apathetic like, "Stuff. Guess I'll do some stuff."

"Have you considered working in ministry? As a pastor or something?"

"Wait...what?" Bewildered. "Me?"

"You're good with your peers, you know how to express yourself, and you seem to have a pretty good handle on your Bible. More importantly, you're a really good kid who seems to love Jesus a lot. Just a thought. Maybe talk to your folks and pray about it."

Beau had simply asked me to think about a possibility. He'd paid attention to those he was shepherding. He'd opened a door and said, "Hey, look in here. Is this how God wants to use you? Maybe. Maybe not. Ask him."

You've got deacons in your church. Godly, capable Christians who love to serve. Imitation-worthy members of the body. Some of them don't even realize what their next step or calling could be. So, while it's Jesus who does the calling, it's often our voices he uses to reach his people. Think and pray about people in the church who you think could be deacons. Don't put pressure on them or force it. Just put the office before them and ask them if the Lord is talking to them. If so, begin the process of discerning with them if God is indeed leading them in that way. You just may have a deacon on your hands. You may have someone who will end up thanking you someday, like I have Beau, for being used to awaken an aspiration to follow God's calling.

Deacon Training

This is already a lengthy chapter, but I want to say a little about training and recommend some additional resources before moving on to some procedures for getting deacons.

- **Training means focused sanctification:** Romans 8:29, 30 says that those whom God predestined, called, and justified are those he sanctifies in order that they'd be *conformed to the image of Jesus*. Train your deacons in the sanctifying process of becoming more and more like Jesus—help them grow in grace.
- **Heart change leads to changes in what we do:** In the time of Ezekiel, the people of God were misbehaving (which was not unusual). What was God's promise to his people, the message he gave his prophet? That he'd give them a new heart and a new spirit—that they'd have a soft heart, and not a hard one (Ezek. 36:26). Train the hearts of your deacons, and the work of their hands will change, too.
- **Learn to discern the difference between sin and mistakes:** You're dealing with deacons in the midst of their sanctification, learning and trying to put into practice the things you're training into them. When a deacon sins, follow church discipline for the restoration of their souls. When a deacon makes a mistake, help them know that retraining isn't the same as rebuking. We want deacons to be cautious of sin, avoiding temptation. We don't want deacons to be afraid of trying their best and

failing—that's where most of the best lessons are learned, anyway.

- **You might not be the best person to develop their competency:** I hit my capacity for developing my first worship leader's skills in ten minutes. Of course, I'm capable of pastoring and discipling him. But as for his particular deaconing skillset? I'm of very little use. Find any and all gospel-centered, biblical resources (books, podcasts, videos, blogs) that you can, and provide them to your deacons. Find godly, competent people and see if your deacons can spend time with them to learn how it's done. Our church is part of the Acts 29 Church Planting Network, and we're fortunate to have had several sister churches nearby who love to train with one another. Basically, don't be the bottleneck to the competency development in your deacons by thinking that you're the one who has to do it all.
- **Theology really does matter:** What you believe about God will determine the way you live. God's Word has power! It's the ammunition the Holy Spirit uses to create gospel transformation in our lives. If you're an elder leading some deacons, this is where you have a chance to shine. Strive to see the

Lord inspire and motivate those you lead toward greater and greater works. Show them the Lord and his gospel over and over. Point them toward the eternal kingdom of Jesus and the role they get to play as deacons. The apostle Peter sought to stir up holy obedience and service to the Lord when he wrote (paraphrased): "Though you haven't seen him, you love him and rejoice! Though you don't see him now, you believe in him and are saved. Be holy and obey the Lord, loving and serving one another!" (1 Pet. 1:8-25). How did these people believe in and rejoice over a Christ they hadn't seen? Peter, by the power of the Holy Spirit, showed Christ to them through the preached Word. Develop the minds and hearts of your deacons with theology—the deep things of God!

- **Deacons learn from teaching *and* doing:** Teach, train, test. Teach, train, test. Lather, rinse, repeat. The classroom isn't just the beginning of training deacons. Start there and go back there constantly. Prepare your deacons for what they'll be doing and what they'll see and experience along the way. But do it knowing that you can't prepare them for everything. So, do your best and then release them to get to work. They're going to have to learn by doing, which will likely mean making some mistakes. That's okay! You've got a deacon with godly character trying to do his or her best to serve! Pull them back, correct, teach, and train. They'll have all sorts of opportunities to exercise beautiful things that should be abounding among God's people: humility, patience, confession, and repentance! If you remove every possibility for your deacons to mess up, then you're totally robbing them of sanctifying opportunities to be more like Jesus.

- **Training doesn't have a finish line:** Village Church Pastor Matt Chandler rightly says, "Sanctification doesn't end in this life. It ends either when Jesus comes back or when Jesus kills you and takes you to heaven." So, if deacon training is really just Christian sanctification, then those who train deacons need to be in it for the lifetime of the deacon.

I was up late one night, watching infomercials. Some extremely hyper guy was hawking this uber-toaster-oven. He kept whipping the audience into a frenzy, repeating, "Set it and forget it!" Apparently, the thing that set it apart was that you could stick your entire chicken in it, set the clock, and walk away without ever checking it again. That's what leaders so often want to do—execute some limited training of deacons, "set" them, and then "forget" about them. Bad idea. Like I said above: teach, train, test. Repeat.

- **Care more about who they're becoming in Jesus than what they're doing for Jesus:** Deacons will trust the training and correction you offer when they know you're not primarily in it to get something out of them. When deacons know your love and commitment for them isn't predicated on their success, but on their value and dignity in Christ, they're more likely to trust you and receive your direction. Essentially, love 'em like Jesus loves you. Pray for them. Pray with them. Inquire about their spiritual walk with the Lord. Demonstrate love for their wellbeing and that of their families. You know . . . be a *pastor*. Your deacons don't need another boss at church—they need a pastor.
- **Serve others before they ever have a chance to serve you:** I'll never forget this one. When I was fourteen, I became the drum major of my high school band and our director sent me to something called the George N. Parks Drum

Major Academy.[23] I had no idea what I was in for. It was there that I met my very first true mentor—the first teacher that I really wanted to be like. While he was teaching a bunch of high schoolers about leading their bands, he was really teaching us how to lead people for the rest of our lives through inspirational service. The first thing he said in our very first session was, "Serve other people before they ever have a chance to serve you." *Boom. My brain exploded.* Don't wait for the deacons in your church to serve you or the church first—be like Jesus and serve them first. Be the first to reach out, first to help them, first to pray for them, first to repent, first to serve. Don't make your training a reactive reciprocation, contingent on the deacon's first move. You open the training by serving them.

23. George N. Parks, director of the UMass Minute Marching Band from 1977 until his passing in 2010. He was also the founder of the Drum Major Academy, which is still educating and training young leaders across the U.S. http://www.drummajor.org.

Training Resources

This isn't a book on leadership training, but I can point you to some good ones. Take a look at some or all of these by better, more experienced leaders and pastors than me.

Books

Leaders Who Last by Dave Kraft

Sticky Teams by Larry Osborne

Leaders at All Levels by Ram Charan

Teaching as Leadership by Steven Farr

You Don't Have to Have a Title to Be a Leader by Mark Sanborn

Podcasts

In the Room With Ryan Huguley (Ryan Huguley, Lead Pastor of Redemption Bible Church)

Rainer on Leadership (Thom Rainer, President of LifeWay Christian Resources)

Andy Stanley Leadership Podcast (Andy Stanley, Lead Pastor of North Point Community Church)

Doctrine and Devotion (Joe Thorn, Lead Pastor of Redeemer Fellowship)

Blogs

http://www.challies.com: Tim Challies, a premier Christian blogger.

http://davekraft.squarespace.com: Dave Kraft, pastor, coach, writer, speaker, and great resources too.

Chapter 5

How Do We Get Deacons?

And the twelve summoned the full number of the disciples and said, "It is not right that we should give up preaching the word of God to serve tables. Therefore, brothers, pick out from among you seven men of good repute, full of the Spirit and of wisdom, whom we will appoint to this duty."

—Acts 6:2-3

They Already Live among Us

Like Agent Fox Mulder, some of you may be saying, "I want to believe."[24] If your church doesn't have anyone serving in the office of deacon, you hope that there are

24. Agent Fox Mulder was the hero (along with Agent Dana Scully) of the '90s Fox sci-fi-conspiracy show *The X Files*. If you haven't watched it . . . do it. *The truth is out there!*

already deacons living among you. I don't have to put on my tinfoil hat to say this: *there probably are.*

Most of us have had the experience of seeing the tried and true folks in the church always serving and always answering the call to help. It can feel like there's only about ten people in the whole church who are doing anything while the rest of the church benefits from their hard work. I'm sorry to say that in so many churches it feels that way because it is that way. Maybe not in your church—if there are contributions from a lot of people, God is greatly blessing your church. Statistically speaking, however, only around twenty percent of the people do the lion's share of the serving and giving.[25] Though that's a shameful statistic, and one that I don't think we should just accept as an unchangeable given, it means that nearly every church has deacons—at least, potentially.

My Diverse Audience

Let's recognize that those of you reading this book come from a wide variety of church governments and structures. Some of you already have an active, biblical diaconate in your church. Some of you have deacons serving on a board, possibly governing in a way reserved for elders. Others reading this are on the front end of installing deacons, either as church planters or existing

25. I believe that when a church rightly institutes the diaconate by God's design, it's in the best position to motivate and challenge the church's people away from this statistical reality!

churches looking to reorient your church's structure. I welcome everyone who's been thinking, *Man, I don't know jack about deacons and didn't know we should have them in our church!* Perhaps there are a few of you who have made it this far and are unconvinced as to the biblical necessity of the office of deacon. God bless you, too—and thanks for sticking with me.

I can't really attempt to address every church's circumstance. That would make for an incredibly long chapter with a lot of my own speculative thoughts, many of which might not translate well in your particular church. My best hope is that you would take what I've offered here—that you'd pray, search the Scriptures yourself, and seek the Holy Spirit's application of his truth in your church.

With that said, I'll take a shot at addressing, in general, those churches who don't currently employ deacons in any official way, as well as those churches with staff members and servants looking to figure out how make the transition to deacons. I have plenty of Scripture to support my views, but I want to be careful with how you receive my recommendations. I can be the pastor of just one church—the one Jesus called me to plant: Restoration City Church. There are so many ways that churches can faithfully institute and employ deacons. My church's way is just one way. It's the one I think is best for us. So the last thing I want you to do is just copy and paste my ideas onto your church.

For instance, when I planted Restoration City Church, I had—literally—no long-term leaders with any ministry experience to speak of. In fact, I spent the first few months of church planting around fire pits, talking to the men and women of my core group, having them explain the gospel to me. Even that was new and challenging to them! What that meant for us, certainly, is that my people didn't have many preconceived notions and assumptions that I'd have to deconstruct. When I said, "Hey! We're orthodox, evangelical, Baptist, reformed Christians!" they all said, "Of course we are, Pastor Matt! What's that mean?" When I said, "It's time for us to appoint some deacons!" they all said, "Awesome, Pastor Matt . . . tell us what to do."[26] But, for some of you, it might take an act of Congress (or God!) to make a significant change.

So the way you should read this section is to think like the moms on the old TV game show *Supermarket Sweep*. Betty, a thrifty, savvy mom of four kids, has the opportunity to careen through a studio grocery store, grabbing up all the groceries she can in just under two minutes. She's dolled up her hair and face for television, and geared up in her most stylish, yet sensible, sweat suit and sneakers. The start buzzer sounds, she burns rubber

---

26. Seriously. That's pretty much how it went. God's been so generous and kind to me as a church planter—I have often looked to the tremendous people who have faithfully planted alongside me and cried with joy and thankfulness.

with her shopping cart—one arm out, sweeping all the groceries she can off the shelf. Milk cartons, loaves of bread, and boxes of floral-scented Tide detergent cascade into the cart. Cart after cart, she indiscriminately loads with grocery goods. It's in the aftermath that she'll thoughtfully pick and choose what she'll keep and use from these carts. Her mission for now? Get everything she can and sort it out later. Follow *Supermarket Sweep* Betty's example. Take everything you can get here and now. Then sort out what could be applied to your church later.

A Possible Protocol for the Church with No Deacons

Regarding the office of deacon, our church's protocol was created and then evolved over the course of two or three years. One of my best friends and brother church planters, Kirk, was out ahead of our church by about ten months.[27] He was just beginning to organize his church's system, and we were doing a lot of church planting work together, so he invited me in to help with the process. The first iteration of Restoration City Church's diaconate came from what Kirk initially created, and then we revised that together.

Over the course of the next several years, I continued to re-evaluate our protocol. What was working? What

---

27. Pastor Kirk McDonald, Gospel Community Church in Fayetteville, GA, http://www.gospelcc.com.

wasn't? What needed help? What needed to be tossed out? Kirk's church continued to revamp it from their end, but as I said earlier, every church is unique and is responsible for faithfully governing its body before the Lord.

At first, a church member aspiring to become a deacon would fill out an application, which I would then review. Attached to the application was a questionnaire/reference from the applicant's community group leader, which primarily covered their character qualifications. If the applicant was good to go, they became a candidate and began a process of theological and ministry development that took anywhere from four months to more than a year. That timeframe depended on how often the candidate was ready to meet with me for coaching, how well they grasped the theology, and their completion of various assignments.

Each candidate was responsible for reading selections from Wayne Grudem's *Systematic Theology*, as well as from Mark Driscoll and Gerry Breshears' *Doctrine*. Along with theological instruction I would ask questions about the candidate's spiritual devotion and development, as well as their current service in the church. Depending on what I learned, I might assign the candidate extra reading or podcast-listening. When their theological studies and additional assignments were completed, they took a big exam. If they didn't pass, I'd put them through remediation and give them another shot. If they did pass, they'd be invited over to my home for dinner with me, my wife, and their spouse (if married) and they'd receive final encouragements and evaluations from me, along with an exit interview.

Phew! Some of you became pastors in your churches with fewer requirements.[28] A few of my trusted Acts 29 pastor bros expressed that same sentiment: "Phew!" In fact, when other pastors learned about our protocol for getting deacons, their reactions were a mixture of awe, curiosity, and doubt. After reading through an early version of my deacon protocol, my friend Keith was sweating and out of breath.[29] "That's quite a lot to put a potential deacon through. It's too much, Matt. Get people who are deaconing into the office of deacon, ASAP." I understood that he wasn't saying to get rid of all qualification or required training—I just needed a better system with a more appropriate, streamlined set of standards and timeframes.

At the same time, I had realized that our church had a big discipleship gap, especially in theological formation. We had many church members who wanted to learn

---

28. You might be thinking, "That's great! We should do that." That's what I mean—it's for the elders of each church to prayerfully approach the Bible and do what seems right to you and the Holy Spirit (Acts 15:28).

29. Pastor Keith Watson, NewCity Church in Macon, GA, http://www.newcitychurches.org.

the Bible and theology that I was teaching the deacon candidates, but they weren't called to the diaconate. So there was all this great teaching and discipleship going on, but lots of people didn't have access to it because that stuff was for the deacons. This realization led to a major shift in our discipleship and deacon protocols.

Keep in mind, we're a young church, planted only five years ago. We were able to start our church with a diaconate. In fact, we had deacons before we ever had any elder candidates to add to our one-elder elder board! Because we're a newer church (and relatively small), we've been able to make nimble decisions. So, as they say in those skin cream commercials that guarantee you'll drop thirty pounds if you slather their product all over you—results may vary.

Our Current Protocol

We ended up making two improvements with one big decision. Everyone at Restoration City Church now has access to our theological discipleship training, and it doesn't take deacon candidates the better part of a year to be installed. We still make sure that we've done our due diligence in testing character and calling, that each deacon is trained and prepared, and that the process only takes about three or four months. I'll put it in an ordered bullet list for ease of reading:

- **Theology Seminar:** Twelve-week course with

selections from Wayne Grudem's *Systematic Theology* as the primary text; lecture and discussion class is once a week for an hour and a half; the twelfth week is an exam which students don't have to take. Students who wish to be evaluated but don't aspire to be a deacon can get a graded exam back. Completing this course and passing the exam is a requirement for all deacon applicants.

- **Application and Community Group Leader Reference:** This is only available for someone who has been a covenant member in good standing for at least four months. It's a basic two-page application, with your community group leader's recommendation; you get a response back within the week.
- **Deacon Candidacy:** A one-month class in which all candidates meet together with an elder. Topics include: calling, instruction on ecclesiology (primarily elders and deacons), character qualifications (with self- and peer-reviewed assessments), spiritual gift profile, personality profile (mainly the DISC assessment), and a current deacon explains what it means to be a deacon in our church.
- **Church Notification and Installation:** Upon completing candidacy, I notify the church from

> the pulpit, and the members are given one week to privately notify me in writing of any disqualifying information about a candidate. If notified, the information is confidentially examined. Otherwise the candidates are installed before the church body on the very next Sunday. We like to make a big deal about this because it is! We bring them up front, teach the church about the diaconate, and call the other deacons and our elders to lay hands on them as we pray over them. These brothers and sisters are then commissioned deacons in our church.

This process shortens the time it takes for a candidate to be installed while still ensuring that character and calling is sufficiently considered, and basic theological training has been completed. We also end up with a deacon season, which basically means we don't have elders or coaches tied up with several candidates at varying stages in the process all year long.

Jesus and His Word Are Permanent, Not Our Church's Protocols

So, that's how we're doing things now: trying our best to be faithful to the Scriptures and aware of our context. If you're thinking, *Wow, you're really bottlenecking the pacing and number of deacons and leaders you're cranking out*, you could be right—that is if we were a bigger or faster-growing church right now. If you're ministering to a church of, let's say, 500 or more, you have the leaders and teachers it takes to possibly run this sort of protocol two or three times a year. You might even need to because your church is growing and the need for deacons is that great. That's just not Restoration City Church's situation right now.

We want to shepherd our leaders and church members to remember that the only thing that doesn't change is the Word of God. Christians can become like the little old lady pack-rat who has a billion and one things stored in her house, most of them collecting dust from decades of negligence. But if you were to touch or move anything, or, God forbid, suggest she get rid of something, she'd flip out! "You can't have a church without a steeple!" "We have to have a choir with choir robes!" "If we don't have a printed church bulletin, how will anyone know who's sick or in need of prayers?" And the list of expectations goes on. It's sometimes hard to change or let go of our beloved systems. And for my too-cool-for-school contemporary brothers, many of us will wring our hands in the decades to come as we worry, *Why aren't there worship song lyrics on the wall? How can a pastor preach if he's not wearing cool jeans? If we don't have a church website or Facebook page, how will people know what our church is like and what we're up to?*

For those of you who are really fired up and want to bring this change into your church (instituting a biblical form of the diaconate), be patient, humble, and kind with those who may push back. I know, I know. "We've always done it that way" isn't a good enough reason to keep doing something. With that said, as a fellow rebellious agent of change, I urge you to please consider that the old, dusty church system or protocol someone's clinging to was probably a faithful Christian's really good idea at some point. And it probably did some good.

So, let's remember that Jesus and his Word don't change, but protocols and systems do. We also need to remember that change can be a painful, scary process for many, so let's be humble, kind, gospel-gracious agents of change, my friends.

The Church with Staff, but Not Deacons

A close pastor friend recently began reaching out, trying to figure out how to incorporate deacons into his church. His is a growing church of around 300 attendees with a little over half of those being covenant members.[30] He's a terribly godly pastor, and he's teamed with four other elders, with two more in-process. He's been a helpful coach and ally to me as a church planter, and I've

---

30. In fact, Tim Bice, lead pastor of Greenbriar Church in Albany, GA (http://www.greenbriarchurch.net), is the one who twisted my arm and made me write this book in the first place. Thanks, Tim. Thanks a bunch.

enjoyed talking biblical deacon concepts with him. He's also a frighteningly adept hunter. Many deer have fallen at his hand. He really is a little scary in his deer bloodlust.

As he and I sat in front of the oversized whiteboard in his office (with many victims of his bow and rifle staring down upon me with lifeless, taxidermied eyes), we brainstormed what his possible plan for deacons should be. We were asking, "How do deacons fit in our church?" The conversation finally became profitable when we asked a different question: "How does our staff fit under God's design for the church?" Tim (That's his name, if you didn't read the footnote!) had a staff of godly people—a church admin, worship leader, youth pastor—the usual suspects. We were trying to figure out what establishing the diaconate at his church could look like when he already had, not just volunteers, but paid, full-time staff members, most of whom aren't pastors. Some of the questions we were wondering about were:

- Should my admin, who's not a deacon, worry about being fired or laid off?
- How much time and energy will it take for all these staff to go through all this deacon training and character testing?
- What positions in my church need to be "rolled over" into the diaconate?
- Should I require every community group leader to be a deacon?

In answering the primary question, "How does our staff fit under God's design for the church?" we recognized that rather than trying to make the diaconate fit into the staff structure, the staff needed to fit into the diaconate. Any non-pastor staff member or servant in the church falls under the broader umbrella term of deacon. Under that umbrella, we then start determining what kind of deacon each person is. For example, his admin serves the church as a deacon. She's essentially already deaconing. The same is true for many others.

So, how to get them to become deacons? That just means some biblical teaching and training for the staff of his church. He gets to spend some time, teaching on the diaconate and then recasting the vision of what the staff looks like under God's design. He's already established the ongoing, healthy rhythm of constant discipleship and training within his staff; he can now simply adjust the curriculum schedule to this area without having to come up with another evening of the week to have extra training meetings.

What about testing their character? That's already been done too! As a good pastor, Tim has selected and hired staff well; he's already measured their character over time and in community. They've been working in ministry, some of them for years, demonstrating their faithfulness and trustworthiness. If anything, he gets to spend some time showing them, from the Bible, how their character already qualifies them as deacons, along with their track record of serving the church.

What about training? What about all that theology, ecclesiology, and personal assessment? As a healthy leadership team, Tim and his staff already meet regularly for fellowship and leadership development. Now, Tim gets to spend a month or two in those ongoing meetings, teaching and training. What's more, before Tim and his elders begin testing, training, and installing deacons throughout the rest of the church, he can pilot his deacon protocol with the staff—all of whom have no reason to be disqualified. At the end of this training season, he can publically install these staff members as deacons, broadcasting the diaconate vision for the entire church.

Should every community group leader be a deacon? The better question to ask, which will answer the first one, is: Which positions should be occupied with deacons? We covered that in the last chapter when we talked about what deacons do. For each church, the elders will need to determine which staff and service positions should be considered deacon-level positions. To review and provide additional clarity:

- Is the position in question a service position? Does the person filling this role directly serve the people of the church? (The answer is almost always yes, but if the position is one that's kind of attached to the church, like the director of a nonprofit the church supports, then possibly not.)

- Does this position wield any authority or level of significant influence over others in the church? If yes, that seems like a lead servant kind of position, especially if they're leading and coordinating deacons under their authority or influence.
- Does this position directly serve the work of the elders (or an elder)? A sermon research assistant, financial counselor, administrator, and ministry team leader (guest services, worship team, etc.) all fit this description.

So, should my community group leaders all be deacons? Yes. No. Maybe. I leave that to the capable judgment of you and your elders. Our elders at Restoration City Church have prayed and determined that the group leader position is a deacon-level position. A very large church of 400 or 4,000 might determine that coaches or leaders of group leaders should be deacons, but that it's not best to require every community group leader (out of the dozens or hundreds you have) to be deacons.

Let's also not forget the option of an "at large" deacon—a qualified Christian member committed to serving the church as a good example who inspires others to serve. That sort of deacon may, for some of you, fill in some of the hard-to-categorize spots in your existing church staff structure.

What a Church like Tim's *Might* Do

Can you tell I really like bullet lists? I'm not a terribly organized person and putting things in bullet lists makes me feel super smart and organized like my wife. Here's the digest-sized version of what a church like Tim's might do—if they already have staff positions and lots of people serving, and they want to realign their church's government and structure to more closely reflect the Bible's design and language:

- Start with the staff first. In the rhythms of your ongoing leadership training and staff meetings, take the time to teach on the diaconate, much like I've been doing throughout this book. Then cast vision for what it should look like in your church.
- Do some thinking and praying ahead of time, preparing to answer some of the more pressing questions your staff and leadership might have.
- Determine which currently existing positions need to be filled by deacons and offer the opportunity to anyone who doesn't have to be a deacon to become an at-large deacon if they feel called.
- In those staff meetings, you might adopt a protocol similar to ours, where you teach and train on ecclesiology, the qualifications

and roles of deacons, how they interplay with elders, and having each staff member assess (or re-assess) their spiritual gifts, their personality, and how they fit within the team.

- At the end of the training and confirmation, have your team help you assess the protocol they went through for the benefit of others in the church who will be going through the same process in the future.
- Publicly install the staff as deacons, and then open the position to aspiring deacons within the church.
- A church like Tim's should also plan to make sure that each deacon has an elder in oversight—whichever elder is responsible for, let's say, guest services, should probably have care and ministry oversight for an at-large deacon who pours coffee.

In addition, a church like Tim's may or may not employ the office of at-large deacon. Larger churches can tend to require far more clearly defined positions and leadership roles. They might opt out of installing at-large deacons who aren't really in charge of any ministry or team. Or, they might opt to employ at-large deacons in the category of leadership development. For example, let's say Tim's guest services leader (a deacon) needs a right-hand person. A go-to guy or girl. If the person he has in mind is qualified, competent, and reliably called to the office of deacon, but won't really be "over" the ministry, they could possibly be an at-large deacon operating in an executive role or in a training (or leadership candidacy) role.

That's just me throwing out some suggestions. As Tim and I have spoken, he and his elders have come up with a host of other questions that I can't hope to include in this book, as much as I'm trying to reach all of you, my diverse audience.

Some of the best help I've received from other leaders and coaches hasn't come from them telling me what to do. Instead, they've shown me what they or others have done as a template for me to consider. They've taught me some principles and overarching truths. It's been up to me (and now, you) to take it or leave it.

The Church with a Deacon Board

This scenario is a lot trickier than others. As I've said previously, I don't believe the Bible teaches us that the church is to be governed and shepherded by deacons. That's for elders to do. If you're reading this right now and you disagree, there are other books I'd point you to for a deeper, more detailed argument. If you're reading this and see the need for your church to shift in governmental organization, I'd say again that you should read other resources, specifically ones regarding the office of elder.

You might not just need a good book about deacons; you may also need a good book on elders. I can't recommend Alexander Strauch's *Biblical Eldership* enough.

The reason I'm shy to speak too much on this scenario is that your church has likely spent years, if not decades, operating under a deacon-led church. It's possible that some of your dearest members' fathers served as governing deacons in your church. There are so many feelings, memories, and traditions involved that a sharp, clear protocol for change will (no matter how biblical) likely bring a substantial level of pain, confusion, and even departures. Initiating or changing something in a newer church is like changing direction on a bicycle. Doing it in a church a decade or two older would be more like trying to change direction in an oil tanker.

There are so many possible factors involved in a church with a deacon board. Some of your deacons may qualify as elders and should therefore be trained and ordained to operate as such. Some of your deacons probably should remain deacons (and be trained and installed into a renewed vision of the diaconate). There are likely some deacons who will disagree fervently with the model I've laid out in this book; they'll have a difficult, but not necessarily impossible, task ahead of them in either making the change or rolling out of their traditional ministry title. For those who must leave the diaconate, you'll want to make that transition as dignified and graceful as possible.

I heard one pastor refer to this sort of scenario as creating a "dignified exit ramp" for those who haven't disqualified themselves in sin, but find that they no longer fit or meet the requirements of a position in the church. You'll want to honor them as much as possible, thank them for their service to the church, and help them figure out how they can best continue serving the church family.

With a transition of this sort, the lead pastor and any agreeable leaders or deacons will need to spend plenty of time establishing buy-in with the church. Take your time, don't rush it, and make sure to listen to the concerns and questions of the folks in your church. Again, many people in the church tend to hold on to traditions, protocols, processes, and offices with a tight grip. If you're in a church with a deacon board that governs rather than one that's elder-governed, this will be tough but worth it.

You'll want to establish a clear vision of the diaconate—the sort of vision I've tried to lay out in this book—to bring to your leaders first. If you're a PowerPoint person, use that. If you like paper documents, use them. They'll want something they can see, read, pray, and ponder over. Bring them God's Word, speak clearly, establish the philosophy of the "why" of the diaconate, and record all of their questions. Schedule a follow-up meeting (or meetings) where you return to discuss possible answers and solutions. This is where the bigger picture concerns about what will happen to your deacon board will come out, which makes sense since you're probably going to be bringing this before the governing deacon board. If you have staff members who lead ministry, but aren't on your deacon board, they'll have a lot of questions, too.

If you can provide a clear, compelling, biblical vision for the diaconate, and if you can garner a trusting agreement that this is a necessary change, you'll begin working out an implementation protocol, which means bringing the vision and philosophy before your church. You'll definitely go through another round of questions and concerns. That's where the patience and grace I spoke about earlier will need to come in. With a deacon board and staff that's already on-board and understand the vision, you'll have more support in laying these things out.

Honestly, I get a little sweaty just thinking about your situation. I'm over here, riding my church-planting bike and you're over there, contemplating how you're going to get this gigantic ship to change direction. Talking to another pastor or leader in a church like yours could be very helpful. Ask a lot of questions. And then ask others to ask the questions you're not asking. Pray a lot. I'll be praying for you, too.

How Many Deacons Do We Need?

Man. I really wish I could tell you. I love answering questions. I'm a leader, and I love teaching and instructing people on what and how to do stuff. As I said, the best I can do here, as in many other places in this book, is offer principles rather than answers.

Remember that every Christian is meant to be a servant. So, in a very real way, every member of your church should view themselves as a noncommissioned deacon. But does it seem sensible (or biblical?) to install every member in the church into the office of deacon? Well, if every single last member of your church has that sort of godly character, competency, and calling, you need to be writing a book and giving interviews on some global news network. You probably don't have that sort of church, though.

With that said, you should try to install enough deacons to ensure that:

1. The ministry of the church is getting faithfully accomplished.
2. The members who serve in ministry are capably influenced and supported.
3. The organization of leadership roles and responsibilities is clear and efficient.

There could be any number of variables that influence that number. Maybe you're a church planting pastor or leader, and out of thirty members you only have one qualified deacon. Or you don't have a lot of ministry positions in your lean, mean church machine—but you have a bunch of qualified, godly servants who aspire to the diaconate. This is going to go right back to your elders' Spirit-empowered deliberations.

Make a Clean Plan, Preparing for the Mess

You organizational, chess-playing, kingly procedure and protocol designers who work so hard to get the right people on the right bus in the right seat at the right time with the right materials know that this is no easy task. There are people with exceptions, extenuating circumstances, strange work schedules, and some who don't quite fit in your system. Fight the urge to purge the "problems" like Colonel Sanders in the second *Matrix*.[31] Be prepared to adjust the protocols you have put in place. There will be people who aspire to the office of deacon who probably should be deacons, and they'll probably just need help working through the system.

I can't offer you the deacon protocol that's just right for your church. I've only tried to offer what the Bible says and then describe some possible templates or routes you might take. The beautiful thing is that you get to study, pray, plan, and then execute something that, if it doesn't work right, you can always tinker with. My church and I are living proof of the need to make adjustments. George Parks, my drum major mentor, often said, "If you fail to plan, you plan to fail." From that, I have derived my own

---

31. Don't tell me the Architect in *The Matrix: Reloaded* doesn't look like a supercilious Colonel Sanders.

saying, "It's better to have a plan that you must change or scrap than to have not have a plan at all."

Whatever you might come up with, don't try to get it perfect. Just aim for biblically faithful. Your plan will probably have to change—indeed, it will almost definitely need to change, especially if your church grows in significant ways. Remember that Jesus and his gospel are permanent, but our systems and protocols can always be changed or replaced.

Chapter 6
What You Can Expect

Count it all joy, my brothers, when you meet trials of various kinds, for you know that the testing of your faith produces steadfastness. And let steadfastness have its full effect, that you may be perfect and complete, lacking in nothing.
—Jam.1:2-4

For those who serve well as deacons gain a good standing for themselves and also great confidence in the faith that is in Christ Jesus.
—1 Tim. 3:13

What *Changes* When a Person Becomes a Deacon?

When Arthur got his sword, he became king. When Peter Parker got his special radioactive spider bite, he became Spider-Man. And Luke Skywalker raided Johnny Cash's closet and became a Jedi.[32] What about when someone who was already serving is installed as a deacon? You lay hands on them, pray over them, publically commission them, and then what?

Should we expect golden, sparkly *shekina dust* to fall down upon them? A shaft of light miraculously imbuing them with a greater measure of the Holy Spirit? Maybe a shiny badge shows up on their chest? Are they given a mysterious scroll to peer into like Po in *Kung Fu Panda*? There's a temptation to think, *When I become a deacon, I'll be promoted;* or *I'll love the church more, once I become a deacon*; or *God will really be pleased with me and I'll become even more spiritual when I become a deacon*. Some of those things may happen. Maybe they should. But what can a newly installed deacon expect to experience?

Deeper Affection for Jesus and His Church

If commitment to Christ and the church isn't already there, you shouldn't be a deacon. We don't seek offices in the church or in ministry in order to find love for Jesus, but because we have love for Jesus. There are so many

32. Okay, so the wardrobe doesn't make young Skywalker a Jedi, but the black outfit really makes his force training come together.

stories of young men pursuing the pastorate because of a deep-seated belief that the love and affection they want to have for Jesus will finally spring up in their souls once they become full-time pastors. Those stories also tend to end in tragedy, as each one who attains the pastorate finds his heart still empty and his soul still searching. Sadly, these men often find out that they weren't responding to a calling. Instead, they were trying to find self-fulfillment in the idol of ministry, rather than finding it in Christ.

But a Christian, with the love of Christ that God himself has placed in his heart, should experience an ongoing increase of love. As the deacon loves what Jesus loves—his church—he'll find himself investing and pouring himself out for it. Whatever we pour our hearts and souls into becomes the focus of our values, desires, hopes, and dreams. When a man pours thousands of dollars into creating the perfect "man-cave," or when a woman spends hundreds of hours on her favorite hobby, his or her identity is often somewhat tied to what other people say about the object of their affection, for the glory it receives reflects back to them.

The blood and the sweat of a deacon mirrors the blood and sweat of Jesus. As the deacon serves the church, he'll grow to care more and more about the church—it reflects his life's purpose. And as the deacon serves the church, he'll learn a greater measure of gratitude for how Jesus loved and bled for him.

Firmer Confidence of Faith

Every Christian questions the reality of his or her faith at some point. "Do I really believe in Jesus? Do I really love him? Or is this just a charade I'm playing for myself and others?" God knew we'd feel this way, so he kindly had the "disciple that Jesus loves" write a letter to us. First John gives amazing reassurance to Christians. It's a helpful diagnostic for the Christian wondering if he or she really believes in Jesus and belongs to him.

There are many gifts God gives to his church to strengthen the faith and assurance of his people. Baptism, for instance, is a good "anchor point" in my memory that keeps my confidence tied to my salvation. It helps me to recall how I felt and thought—the sense of faith conviction—when I was baptized. *I believe in Jesus and love him truly. I want everyone to know about how he's saved me. In fact, I'm willing to be publicly dunked underwater to show it!* For some whom I've pastored through a lack of assurance, I ask them to go and look at their giving records.[33] Have you placed faith in Jesus as your Savior

---

33. This is not a reassuring, confidence-building exercise for the Christian who isn't generous to the Lord. This isn't to say you should only call on faithful givers to look at their giving because they'll feel better about their faith. A faithful pastor might be doing a struggling Christian a favor by having them see and be convicted by their pattern of giving, and thereby be drawn to repentance and renewed faith. "For where your treasure is, there your heart will be also" (Matt. 6:21).

and Lord? Do you see all of that worldly wealth you've handed over to him and his purposes? Money you could have spent on yourself and the trinkets and pleasures of this life? You've literally put your money where your mouth is (your profession of faith)!

So, too, the deacon can, in times of struggling over the genuineness of his or her faith, look upon a record of service and have good evidence that they truly have been believing in and loving Jesus. Of course, just looking at your works isn't a guarantee that your faith is true. Jesus says as much in his parable of those who will show up in heaven on the Last Day, pointing to all the good works they did in his name. Jesus will tell these people, "Guys, I don't know you—we're not friends. You did that stuff in my name, but you didn't do it because you loved me. You built a name for yourself with my name. You built your reputation and wealth on my name. You didn't love me—you used me! Get out of here and go where you belong" (see Matt. 7:21-23).

With that said, with prayer and sincere pleading for the Lord to show you evidence of heart change by works, the deacon can find a reason to have confidence in their faith. The Lord has given you a heart of service that makes his name increase (John 3:30).

Development of Skill through Training and Experience

I grew up in the world of video games. I largely refused

the traditional life of young boys playing baseball and football, hunting and fishing, and earning merit badges on their Boy Scout sashes. Instead, I devoted myself to the art of swordplay, spell-casting, and *pwning n00bz*[34] in video games.

What I learned in video games is that it takes time and effort to get more proficient—to learn your way around a map, gain skill points, get more experience—and you have to keep leveling up to meet the challenges that lie ahead. That lesson taught me a bit about life, and I think it has an application for deacons in the church.

Over time, a deacon should be developing and training continuously in his ministry to the church. Your competencies for serving as a deacon were given to you by the Lord and it's your responsibility to put them into practice and grow into them. Many will equate these things with "spiritual gifts"—abilities that God grants through his Spirit for serving the church and evangelizing the lost. That takes time and many attempts. You can only sit in the classroom, listening to lectures and reading books, for so long. At some point, you have to put it all into practice.

---

34. A "n00b" is anyone you can beat and then mock in a video game. "Pwning" just means you're able to defeat them a lot. You've really pwned someone if they disconnect from the game and fling their controller against the wall (referred to as "rage-quitting"). Video gamers have some serious bullying and self-control issues. Y'all pray for them.

Over the course of the years that a deacon faithfully serves, he or she should improve in his or her ability to serve. Perhaps the first time you were called on to greet people in the lobby, shake hands, and go through the welcome information visitors need, you found it nerve-wracking and you may have only done half of what you were taught to do. But now your handshake is sure, your smile warm, and your conversation with visitors is smooth and full of helpful information about the church. With experience and ongoing training, the deacon should expect to get more proficient and skilled.

Greater Appreciation for Those Who Serve and Have Served

Sometimes it takes doing what others make look so easy to learn that it's not that easy. When I was a freshman in the high school band, the drum majors looked like they had the easiest job ever—and then I became the drum major and I learned otherwise. Same with teaching high school. Same with becoming a dad. Same with pastoring.

A deacon will learn soon enough that serving and being welcomed into greater influence or authority means more responsibility. Longer hours. More care and concern. All in service to many people who just don't get what it takes to make the things of the church happen. New deacons in my church often say to me that they didn't realize that there's just so much to do! They also express newfound appreciation for those who have come before them, as well as for those they work alongside.

I've heard pastor Matt Chandler of the Village Church describe how pastoring can feel like being a shepherd who, "while most of the sheep are all playing volleyball and having a barbecue, we're on the outskirts of the party, tending to the sick sheep. Oh, and they're rabidly biting us." Deacons will understand that to a great extent too. A deacon will come to appreciate and be thankful for everyone who serves Jesus's church, knowing that it's not nearly as glamorous as it can look from the outside.

Growing Sturdiness and Steadfastness

Have you ever been in a fight? I've been in one or two. In your first one, everything's happening so fast. It's a blur of fists, feet, (possibly teeth!)[35] and so much noise. There's so much stimuli coming at you, with not a lot of time to figure out what's happening. Add a ton of adrenaline flooding into your system and you realize that fights don't really work out like Jean-Claude Van Damme movies. It's like the fight turned the volume in the world up to *eleven.* For someone who's had some experience fighting (on the street or in the ring), time starts to slow down a bit—they can start to "read" the situation. The volume gets turned

35. Depends on who you fight. If it's me, I'll probably try to bite you. If it's some of the toddlers in my church, they're definitely biters. "But who fights toddlers?" you might ask. Don't ask questions you don't want answers to . . .

down and they can manage the stimulus of a stressful situation better.

For a lot of people in the church, when something bad or dramatic happens, it's like the volume of the problem is staggeringly loud and they can't think of anything else. Part of the job description of the deacon is to solve problems and deal with difficulties, which means new deacons will have to deal with increased volume levels in their lives. It can be pretty distracting, trying to serve people and working hard to manage the increased responsibilities you have.

After a while, deacons will find that the volume of drama and difficulty won't be nearly quite so loud. A deacon should start to see that not everything that once seemed like a church-destroying problem actually is. Sturdiness, one might call it. A deacon will become a bit sturdier over time. As they say, "a smooth sea never made a skillful sailor."

Imagine the sturdiness Paul gained after the seventeenth time he tried preaching in front of a hostile crowd or the umpteenth time some guys gave him a beatdown. When someone complained to Paul that the color of the auditorium carpet in Corinth was bad, I'm sure he didn't wig out. James assures us that "trials of various kinds" test our faith and "produce steadfastness." He urges us to let that sturdiness, or steadfastness, "have its full effect" (Jam. 1:2-4). A deacon will have plenty of opportunities to be made "steadfast."

Expect and Celebrate Change

Other things about the deacon and his experience in the church and life can change as well. Much of it will come from some un-fun experiences. Some of it will come from some awesome, happy experiences. Either way, we celebrate and pray for Jesus to sanctify us through serving his church in the midst of change. Try not to let this stuff take you by surprise, but trust that God puts these changes to good use—for our joy, the health of our churches, and for his glory.

The Reward of Good Work

In John Piper's book *Desiring God,* Piper addressed a commonly held view in Christianity that doing good works as an act of loving others isn't truly good or truly loving if the worker of good is motivated by personal gain. In fact, after preaching on his biblical perspective of "Christian hedonism," Piper had a philosophy professor criticize him in a letter, writing:

> Is it not the contention of morality that we should do the good because it is the good? . . . We should do the good and perform virtuously, I suggest, because it is good and virtuous; that God will bless it and cause us to be happy is a consequence, but not the motive for doing it.[36]

---

36. John Piper, *Desiring God* (Multnomah Publishers, 2003). If you haven't read Piper's book, put mine down, go buy a copy, and then come back to this when you're done. Seriously.

You can read Piper's full response in *Desiring God*. What I'll say here, in brief, is that I agree with Piper: the professor gave a patently unbiblical critique. First Timothy 3:13 indicates a motivation for the deacon to serve and serve well (a good standing and great confidence). Jesus himself attaches the assurance of treasures in heaven to his command to obey him and serve. Part of the motivation the Bible gives us to do good works (in this case, deaconing for the church) is for the personal joy and satisfaction we gain in doing so. It's not wrong to seek gain by loving others—it's wrong to seek the wrong kind of gain—selfish gain. Indeed, Jesus tells James and John (and their meddling mom!) that, if you're motivated to be first, then you should seek to become last. He doesn't rebuke them for their motivation toward reward—the problem is with how they intend to get it (see Matt. 20:20-28).

There are honorable rewards the deacon should seek to gain by serving the church, two of which are specified by Paul in 1 Timothy 3:

1. "A good standing for themselves…"
2. " . . . and also great confidence in the faith in Christ Jesus."

A Good Standing

"Well done, good and faithful servant" (Matt. 25:21,23). That's what you want to hear from the Master when you are greeted in heaven. That's what I call motivation. I can speak for every child who yearned and ached for the approval of his or her father. To be told, "Good job!" by the one you admire, love, and respect the most is incredibly important. People have spent their entire lives and careers seeking the approval of their parents, bosses, and the world around them, and too many of them either never receive it or are never satisfied by it. The deacon, however, is assured of this reward from our Heavenly Father—a good standing—for serving well.

Now, this will be the inheritance of every Christian—the approval of our Father, purchased by the perfect work of Jesus on the cross. But there is an apparent hierarchy of rewards in heaven, established by our works in this life. To the deacon who serves well, there is an eternal standing—a reputation—that comes to him or her.

It should be reasonable to expect that in addition to an eternal, heavenly good standing, a faithful deacon should expect to receive a good standing in his or her church. The dignified character of a deacon, along with serving well, should bring about a general good reputation within the body. If a deacon is someone who the church can point to and say, "Imitate that person, as they imitate Jesus," that obviously indicates they're someone who's serving well for the sake of Christ. And that's a great motivation—to be honored for Christlike service.

A Great Confidence in Your Faith

As we said earlier in the chapter, devoted servant-followers of Jesus—deacons—will experience great confidence in their faith. In other words, a deacon will discover the great reward of boldness, freedom, a clean conscience, and fulfillment as they "work out [their] salvation with fear and trembling" as God works in them for "his good pleasure" (Phil. 2:12, 13).

To know that you are who God intends for you to be, doing what God intends for you to do is quite a reward! This kind of reward empowers the serving work of a deacon. Imagine a good boss rewarding one of his good mechanics with a brand new, top-tier set of tools to do his work. Or a great ballerina receiving new gear from her instructor. A deacon who serves well is rewarded great confidence in his faith in Christ—a faith that strengthens the deacon to continued, joyful service.

Bonus Reward

Like a great composer enjoying his audience's enjoyment of his masterpiece, a deacon may find some reward in seeing the fruit of his ministry labors:

- To see church members fellowship in a clean, well-maintained facility
- To see church members worship freely with a well-led, organized, Spirit-led worship team

- To see guests welcomed with coffee, warm smiles, handshakes, and new friendships
- To see children taught by coordinated, trained teachers with an organized curriculum
- To see church elders helped in prayer and administrative assistance
- To see the sick and lonely visited, encouraged, and loved
- To see people in the community reached with both true words and sacrificial works
- The deacon will find enjoyment and fulfillment and a sense of wondrous satisfaction in what the Lord has called and empowered him or her to do. There's something extraordinarily pleasing that happens in our hearts when we fulfill the calling and role God gives us.

I once heard a pastor explain the dynamic of serving the Lord in ministry, along with the emotional reward of doing so:

> When I was a kid, my dad, who worked in construction, took me to work with him. It was the best. I put on my blue jeans and a plain white tee shirt, just like the one my dad wore. My mom packed me a lunch in a box, just like the one she made for my dad every morning. We rode in his truck, picked up his

> work buddies, and headed to the job site.
>
> When we got to my dad's work, I got out my set of "kids' tools" and wailed away on scrap pieces of wood and drywall. I made a lot of messes. I didn't actually accomplish anything close to the work that my dad was doing. I often got in the way of him and his work buddies. But none of that mattered. To me, it was the best day. And I know it was the best day for my dad because he told me so all day long. It wasn't the best day because of all the work I did (which was nothing)—it was the best because my dad brought me along and he let me do work with him. That's ministry.[37]

Without a doubt, that's the best analogy I've ever heard regarding the work of ministry. It's awesome, liberating, and encouraging to me. I want every deacon who serves well (or simply serves the best he or she can) to experience the reward of having been invited on to their Heavenly Father's work site to think, feel, and act like him. That's a great reward!

---

37. Mark Driscoll, Lead Pastor, Trinity Church, Scottsdale, AZ.

Conclusion

God is not unjust so as to overlook your work and the love that you have shown for his name in serving the saints, as you still do. And we desire each one of you to show the same earnestness to have the full assurance of hope until the end, so that you may not be sluggish, but imitators of those who through faith and patience inherit the promises.
—Heb. 6:10-12

Leadership through Serving like Jesus

If I were to ask you if you want to be like Jesus and you're a Christian, the answer would obviously be yes. The proof of whether you meant it, though, would be if you served like Jesus. The church is the instrument of gospel proclamation—through the words of Jesus and the works of Jesus. When people encounter a church full of Christians who lay down their lives in serving one another and serving the lost, they get a vibrant picture of the gospel.

I think that's what the apostle Paul meant when he said he's "filling up what is lacking in Christ's afflictions for the sake of his body, that is, the church" (Col. 1:24). The church in Colossae was made up of many who hadn't met Jesus personally, face-to-face. They hadn't been there to see Jesus before them, crucified and dying on a Roman cross. It's not that there was anything "lacking" in Christ's sufferings, leaving anything necessary unfinished. Instead, the only thing Paul sees as lacking is that Jesus isn't right here, physically with us, suffering for us to see with our own eyes. What Paul's "filling up" means, then, is serving and suffering like *Jesus* in front of the Colossians. If more Christians were willing to imitate Paul as he imitates Jesus's path of sacrificial service, we'd see a healthier, more robust church whose gospel proclamation carries more power.

I started this book by identifying a great problem in the church today—so many people say they want to be like Jesus, but far too few are willing to suffer and serve like him. I dare say that has led to a host of symptoms of illness in much of American Christianity. It's led to very small percentages of the church giving and serving and maintaining the ministry while a very large percentage of the church passively looks on, disengaged and ineffective. But I don't want to just point out the problem and say, "Look at this. This is wrong." Anybody can point out a problem but not too many are willing to work on the solution.

Step Up and Lead through Serving

Elders and deacons, listen up! Our churches need to obey Jesus and walk in his design. We need Christians who will lead by example, encourage with their words, and accomplish Christ's service through hard work. We need men and women who will take the wealth of spiritual gifts God has given them and leverage these for the body. We need men and women with godly character and deep commitment to Jesus and his people, using their influence and authority for righteousness and unity.

As an elder of a church, I can tell you that I sympathize with Jerry Maguire, as he stands before a crowded office, lays out his crazy vision for the future, and then—wild-eyed and desperate—asks, "Who's comin' with me?"[38] For what seems like an eternity, no one says a word. They just stare. And then Dorothy Boyd[39] stands up and says, "I'll go!" Relief. Hope. Encouragement. I'm not alone in

38. The main character of the movie by the same name, played by Tom Cruise.

39. Tom Cruise's love interest, played by the adorable Renee Zellweger.

this—someone's going to step up, follow, work, and even lead others with me. Someone's got to step up and say, "There's work to do. We can do it because we're called to do it. We have the God we need and we have his Spirit. Let's lace up our boots and get to it!"

I'm Talking to You

I know many of you who are pastors are thinking it would be life-changing for you and your church if you had some people step up and commit to serving like that. Or maybe you're not a pastor but someone aspiring to lead in your church. Or maybe you're a member of a church, troubled by what seems to be a lack of servant-leadership. Whatever roles or titles you have, I'm glad and grateful you're reading this book. I want to challenge you now, though. I think there's a burden of responsibility when you receive information and instruction—a call to respond to the message. And I think you will respond in some way. You'll either apply what you've learned (maybe not everything I've told you, but you'll move in action!), or you'll put this book down and keep doing what you've always done, somehow hoping for different and better results (but not seeing them).

The apostle James says that if we encounter God's Word and fail to live by it, we're like someone who's seen his natural face in a mirror and then walked away, forgetting what he looked like (Jam. 1:22-25). I've tried to show you what our churches often look like, as well as what they should and could look like—churches with real, powerful, humble, godly deacons who serve the body and proclaim the gospel through their works.

I'm talking to you, Pastor, Deacon, and whoever else is reading this. Please respond. Think about what I've shared with you. Pray and ask God to reveal his truth from the Bible. Talk with your elders. Talk with potential deacons. Read this book together and discuss it. Dream of what your church could look like when served by a fully engaged biblical diaconate. I'm not just talking to you, though; I'm praying for you too. I'm rooting for you and your churches. Prayerfully make plans and put things in motion. Call people to be like Jesus by serving like Jesus.

Acknowledgments

I always figured I'd write a book, but I never thought it would be one about deacons. Even though this book has but one writer, it couldn't have come about without a number of people who just happen to be my favorite people.

First, thanks goes to my family—Shannon, Maggie, Molly, and Martin—who believe in me, encourage me, and let me lead them, even though they have a front row seat to my follies and failures. Thank you for trusting me and loving me.

Second, not only my thanks but my admiration goes to my mom, Dr. Barbara Ford, who's inspired me and sacrificed so much to see me chase my dreams and callings. Also, I want to express my appreciation for my dear dad, Larry, who's worshiping even now at the feet of Jesus. Dad, you were a man who did nothing but serve his family. I'm so glad I got to be pastor to both you and Mom.

Next, my gratitude goes to my brothers and sisters in the faith—the Restoration City Church family. Thank you for not only growing in Christ but for giving your pastor grace, patience, and plenty of room to grow alongside you. You've taught me so much about shepherding and leading. This book is in large part a testimony of what I've learned from you. Special thanks to John and Emily Poss, and Christian and Maiya Wall, who read the manuscript and provided invaluable feedback.

Thanks, also, to Tim Bice, who wanted deacons in his church, invited me to spend a weekend with him to share what I'd learned, and then tricked me into writing a book under the pretenses of teaming up to do it. Seriously—I got two chapters in and you said, "You got this, bro. Run with it." I can't thank you enough for getting me on this path to writing and publishing and for being a truly wise and faithful role model.

To Kirk McDonald, who has been nothing if not a pastor's pastor, I offer my thanks. I could write a book solely about what sort of influence you've had on my life. Suffice it to say, this book wouldn't have happened if you hadn't invited me to join you in learning about deacons and implementing them in our church plants.

To Jesus, thank you for laying down your life in service to your church. You, who, for your glory, brought us joy and freedom from slavery to our sin and shame, are worthy of praise and thanksgiving. I owe you an eternal gratitude for leaving your throne to become as one of us. You showed us what it looks like to make yourself a humble servant; you are the true pastor, the true deacon, the one true Son of God. All glory be to you, forever.